Maine Metaphor

Maine in Winter

Maine Metaphor

Maine in Winter

S. Dorman

Foreword by John Wilson

RESOURCE *Publications* · Eugene, Oregon

MAINE METAPHOR
Maine in Winter

Resource Publications
An Imprint of Wipf and Stock Publishers
199 W. 8th Ave., Suite 3
Eugene, OR 97401

www.wipfandstock.com

PAPERBACK ISBN: 978-1-7252-8745-7
HARDCOVER ISBN: 978-1-7252-8744-0
EBOOK ISBN: 978-1-7252-8746-4

02/17/21

In Loving Memory of Harold and Jean

Contents

Foreword

"Nothing can permanently please, which does not contain in itself the reason why it is so, and not otherwise." I bristle reflexively at such sweeping aesthetic pronouncements, but this one from Coleridge (which I first encountered as a freshman in college in the fall of 1966) stands up pretty well. It comes to mind because I've just finished reading (and re-reading) the book you're holding in your hands: S. Dorman's *Maine in Winter*, a collage of journal entries (some from the early 1990s, more from November 2009 into February 2014), wide-ranging ruminations, and narrative (see the section wryly headed "Personal Recreation," one of the best accounts of a sudden, wrenching injury and its immediate aftermath that I've ever encountered).

In one entry, from December 18, 2009, Dorman writes:

> Ever notice, reader or writer, the vast difference between how a story is *told* versus how one's story is lived? It is almost as though God's taste in stories seems to gloss the high points and is mostly comprised, instead, of detritus. I don't understand why God doesn't get bored. Take the reading of blogs.

Dorman then quotes a brief and remarkably banal blog entry and remarks, "God must love this stuff—there's so much of it. We just don't realize it, but we are the greatest story ever told." She ends this passage with an ironic resolution: "I plan no more online commenting."

The irony derives from a tension that's built into her project. Dorman wants to capture the quicksilver nature of our lives, the way that everyday routines and sights and sounds and smells of what we call "the natural world" are intertwined with an intense awareness of God—the God who utterly exceeds our grasp and yet at the same time reveals himself to us, makes us aware of his incomprehensible love. To do this, she must be faithful to the quotidian without falling into the narcissistic tedium of that blog entry; equally, she must be faithful to the "showings" she receives without seeming to float away into the aether.

And she succeeds magnificently. *Maine in Winter* is a miscellany, a form that I love, part nature-journal (unsentimental, but all the richer for that), part domestic chronicle (with very appealing glimpses of a long and happy marriage), part spiritual journal, part a chronicle of reading, part a reflection on writing (with wry observations on her own aspirations and the vicissitudes she's endured)—all this and more.

I already have in mind a shortlist of people I'll be giving a copy of this book to; I suspect that you will too, when you've finished *Maine in Winter*.

John Wilson

Little Winter

Seth Invites Me Hunting

"Do you still want to go hunting with me?" Seth asked me last night.

This morning at 7:30 we walk up Deer Hill Road together, me trying to match my quicker paces to his long languorous ones. He is maybe 6 ft. 3 in., dressed in denim and flannel, soon to vest himself in hunter's blaze orange; cradling Allen's new walnut stock Winchester 30–30 in the crook of his left arm. This son is two months out of his teens.

When we reach the power line he dons the vest and loads brass shells into the chamber, each clicking into place. We start off over frost-stiffened ground, each brown leaf and fern blade finely etched in delicate whiteness. Then I notice my sneakers and Seth does too. He gives me a sorry glance and smiles. My feet will be soaked when the frost comes out of the ground, drawn by a sun that is even now rising among these low mountains.

We crunch along through puckerbrush; he points to thickets of tall thin saplings and tells me he saw a doe in there last week. I'm not worrying, Seth has no doe permit. We follow the power line down and already our feet are kicking up silvery water droplets. At the base of this hill a swamp glimmers, its stream running through.

Seth asks, low, if I want to cut with him into woods on the left across the rocky stream. I nod my assent. Unthinking, I step on several beech branches, cracking, and he gives me a look.

Stepping through woods we make for the great purple-gray rock face. I notice a ceramic pot shard as we move through frosty leaves. There may be other remnants of an old homestead nearby. We cross a stream immediately below the rock face and Seth stops to listen. This is where I saw telltale brown droppings a few weeks ago. Our backyard is not far from here; we are in the country of deer.

I travel behind several paces, stopping when he stops that he might better hear the sound of his prey. Still coming alongside the stream, and, picking my way over rocks, I grab a thin birch trunk; it snaps clean, crisp yellow wood showing. I wince at the noise, wonder at breaking such a healthy young tree.

I come through, bright in hunter's orange, wearing a white stocking cap, toting Seth's duffel bag and noting things on 3 x 5 cards . . . I come through a woods choked with thin trees. Everywhere we look we see twigs, stems of thin tall trees from a cutover: thickets of fine cover for gray deer, brown deer, tan. Their coats will be turning to winter gray.

Having skirted round to its end, we climb part way up the back of great rock, stepping over rivulets of water, over downed trees, red rotten deadfall glistening with fine lines of frost. Lanky Seth motions for me to stop taking notes, catch up with him.

"Want to see some bear sign?"

I nod vigorously.

"Right there." He points, but I see nothing, just some leaves and debris.

"Where?" (Whispering.)

He points again, gesturing round. And slowly I see. Leaves have been disturbed by scrapings, gouges, the dirt dug up in a rut here, a circle over there. The might of bear shows in riven earth.

"He was looking for food, probably grubs."

As we come down the rock toward a section of marsh, Seth points to densest thickets. I see a flicker of white, maybe a brown movement, hear the crackling of brush and my own voice saying, "I see it!"

He has already brought Allen's 30-30 up, but takes it down quick. Had I the gun I might have shot, but for one thing. Instantly—in my mind along with that volatile desire to shoot at the white flag of a deer—came the memory of Karen Wood.

And with that memory I take off my white hat. For me, since the death of Karen Wood, white stands for target because it stands for deer. The 27-year-old mother of infant twins was shot to death two years ago in her Bangor area back yard during deer season. The man who shot her "saw deer" (so it was formally adjudicated). But the white flag of the deer turned out to be white mittens on Karen Wood, keeping her hands warm while hanging clothes on the line in her yard. Seth does not shoot this deer because he sees no rack. ". . . I think it was the doe I saw before."

You see the conundrum.

Hunters without doe permits may not shoot unless they see a legal rack—antlers of more than three or four inches. A hunter, shooting at a moving white target, may be shooting somebody's mother, whether cervine or human, the first with a legal penalty, the other without. If I hunt I must keep Karen Wood and the image of her infants, and of her white mittens flickering among trees, uppermost in my mind. *If I hunt?*

So I remove my white stocking cap and turn the white lining of the coat I carry. And, walking on, I think about the fluffy white flag of that retreating doe. I think also of my son's restraint and level-headedness.

Seth tells me we are going up to "my spot," to sit and wait for a buck to come along. But first we stop beside a large lichen-covered rock to don scent. And scent remover. His method is to put the stinky strong stuff of cervine hormones to the soles of our shoes, then spray scent-remover over our legs so we won't leave human horror-stink on the trees and bushes as we brush past.

We go up, the sun has too. Seth pointing out fine tracks in leaf mold that I would have missed "where they come down." He has scouted the area and knows their habits on slopes below the rock sides of Swans Ledge.

We begin climbing in earnest, stopping to remove orange vests, strip off some clothing, and put our vests on again. The slope is rocky with talus off its ledge—frost wedging is delicate yet mighty in breaking rock into fragments. On our way down he instructs me to walk on the rocks: it's quieter. We spy black droppings—like round pellets—they are fairly fresh . . . but not so fresh? The first batch is frosted, the second slick with water. We disagree. I say they aren't frosted so are more recent. But the sun has thawed them. Seth points out frost on the edges.

Now with a climb comes sweat and laboring. The slope is a field of gray rocks, interspersed with the twiggy clutter of trees pointing skywards. Finally he brings me out to a grouping of large rocks, instructs me to settle in while he does a little more scouting. There's a place, a bit below, where he's seen much sign. He wants to go down here in those large rocks.

I spread the gray coat I've been carrying between a couple rocks upon leaf mold and sit down. It feels good to recline, the sun level in my eyes. I'm on a height of lookout, and just below Swans Ledge. Looking across the valley I see the town mountain, gray and brown, rutted with ski trails; and the shimmering surfaces of ponds.

Seth returns and tells me he's discovered the deer equivalent of bathroom. "The scent is wicked powerful there. I can smell it here, can you?" Until I start putting these words down, it does not occur to me to wonder of the possibility that hunters were there, and likewise artificially scented.

We both settle in. I close my eyes and listen for sounds one might hear in these woods. First I notice an irritation—chirruping of a squirrel; a swishing of its movements in the duff. I hear rattling of leaves over the forest as a slight breeze blows. I begin noticing sounds more distinct but persistent, pervasive: traffic on the two-lane to Portland, banging of lids at the town dump mistaken for gunshots until Seth informs me otherwise. A jet screams by in the east; a constant distant murmur of machinery from roadwork drifts up, a saw working in woods across the valley below the town mountain. Everything man-made now, noisy. Yes. This is not the Allagash woodland. This is our neighborhood.

Would I come up here if I were a deer?

But they do. They cross and re-cross, traverse the area. Alive.

Our sky has begun to cloud over, our sun is a bright spot in clouds . . . Sweat of the climb clings and chills. I put on more clothes, my mittens, even the hat.

I sit up and strain sight into the thickets, intent.

But there would be no buck today. Two teenagers come crackling through, smoking and talking, cradling guns.

Brook Wight

It is 36° at 8:30 a.m. on this early November day, a seasonal temperature. Yesterday at this time it was 60 degrees; at 2 p.m. it was 71.6°F. In the morning Allen and I drove toward the foot of Step Falls. On a perfect summer of an All Saints Day. The atmosphere still, warm, mute, the sun softened in a cloud-washed sky.

As we came on in the Subaru we looked up at white landslide on the side of a dark mountain. Perhaps 1200 to 1500 ft. patch of white, striated with brown, it was a new scar, an intriguing effacement, water-washed wound of rock. What might one find there, so high in the forest? Great old timber toppled to a mere pile of sticks. And who knows what else? Only those who have bushwhacked, only those who have climbed. And what are they are finding, those who have gone in search of gems? This, I disclose to the page, is beryl country. But I'm more interested in metaphors. What would I find if I dared to climb to the landslide?

We parked below among conifers and began to hike in the warm brown November woods. Brown, brown and then the dark green. The grays and whites of the trunks. And near, through trees, the running stream of Wight Brook—named for an early settler perhaps—white in peripheral vision, but noisy, not peripheral to our ears. In places the ground was springy with humus, with old needles and leaves, but we found also the roots of trees protruding, lacing and interweaving a forest floor tamped by the feet of hikers. We passed a prone deteriorating pine, mossy and old, split lengthwise as though with lightning. It was full of great holes, gift of the woodpeckers and bugs. In the small ravines—rocks green with lichen and mold.

Allen and I continued to look for and occasionally site the distant landslide through these trees. At times it appeared, at times not. We talked about climbing it, about *how* to climb it.

"Take a site with the compass," said Allen. "Look through trees toward the slide and align the compass needle with that orientation of the slide."

"I can do that."

"And you can use obvious landmarks. See that white birch, the furthest one? Site on successive landmarks."

The path curved, or was it the stream that curved? And we saw above distantly the white pouring steps of the brook, Wight Brook. The rocky cataracts of Step Falls.

We climbed higher and came upon an old iron pipe, rusting away near the boisterous falling stream, taken apart by oxygen-rich water. The human-made thing—this pipe—was not like any I'm familiar with. I didn't check its diameter but it may have been eight or ten inches. Too large, Allen speculated, for a purely domestic water supply. It'd been made by wrapping and riveting long sheets of iron into a spiral, whorled with iron rivets about an inch apart on center, a third of an inch from edge to edge of each rivet.

We stood wondering over the pipe, which extended down into the woods out of sight.

"We could tell when it was in use if we knew when this type of manufacture was prevalent," I offered. Later I would remember that there'd been a timber settlement here in the Notch, early in the century, complete with mill and all things necessary to settlement life. Grafton Notch settlement, that would be. They gave up on it when the timber was gone: rocky, cold, close between mountains, no place to farm.

Allen straddled the cold pipe and sat down. He fell to wondering again.

I went to the edge of trees bordering Wight brook and walked out onto rocks beside the hollering flood. Here were great smooth granite rocks beneath the grip of my sneakers. Some were broken by immane force. In others a white width of quartz intruded, snaking. Whiteness shone brightly beneath the falling stream.

Allen joined me momentarily on the rocks and we ascended at varying paces. He was soon out of sight above me. I climbed till I came to those smooth natural slides folks love on hot days. We too had slid down in cut-offs through spray on such summer days. Water had modeled these rocks, almost to a polish. It fell greenly and foaming into pools, the green like a precious gem, the foam white-green and sprightly,

Spritely. Water wights. Raucous and whirling. A bridge of dense continuous spray shot up off a lip of rock, curving into the air, smiting further rocks; continually. Here were movement and mineral life, tugged by gravity shamelessly wrecking the elements.

Allen hailed me through this roaring from an opposite shore of rock above, gesturing to follow him. He had crossed a narrow place in the stream, wading in work boots with thick black soles. I took off my sneakers, stuffed them with pink socks and waded in. November. My feet began cramping in these cold mountainous waters. The rock beneath was slick with algae. He grasped my upheld arms and lifted me onto his rock.

We climbed still higher and plopped down on a ledge leaning out over this flood. Allen lay down on his back and I sat staring upstream—alternately observing and absent in thought. Finally I looked over at him and watched only him.

"What are you looking at?" My voice was raised above the shout of the brook.

His was too. "I'm looking into heaven."

"What are you thinking about?"

"I was listening to and thinking about the noise of the water."

I'll try that, I thought.

I lay on my back beside him on cool rock and closed my eyes. What does the water say?

On my right, upstream, it made a lighter shallower sound than the sound off to my left, downstream. Rocks stepped shallowly up the stream, flooding broader and flatter. Downstream steps were steeper, the flood narrower, falling deeply, resonant. I caught the voice of both at once, left ear and right. The sounds, I thought, are like those of varying distant winds in woods; one is mightier than the other in its flaw.

As if in answer, a wind from above fanned my face and whispered in passing. Well, maybe they are not like the voice of the wind. To wind, no doubt, the water sounds different. But when did the breeze gets here? Can the atmosphere be changing? Is water-weather moving in?

I came out of that drowsing speculative state to hear Allen asking if I were ready to descend. I turned onto my belly and peered over the edge of rock into water, traveling calmly beneath it. Here it made no noise I could discern. It was clear, revealing the brown and green of soils and gravel and algae on a more level surface.

You are silent, moving, I thought.

"I'm ready now," I said, and stood.

We decided to re-cross Wight Brook while still upon this height. In furthest sight, spread the dark great bulk of Old Spec, hazed in a juxtaposition of itself and the sun.

Allen caught me twice as I jumped from stone to stone over the broad split stream. It was not usual, this helping me across moving water. I decided to remember it and mark it down in my journal later.

Then we saw the logging road leading away from the shore. We could take it down for a change, but . . . where would we come out?

To be certain of reaching our car, we took a path marked by white blazes along the trunks of trees. The trees of beech and cedar and fir, hemlock and spruce and pine.

Nearing the bottom again, we saw splintered white remains of some old tree, falling apart in the ground, becoming ground itself, no longer having any but the most unbecoming form of "tree." Only the woody fibers hinted at its former state. A tree becoming ground, its former cradle. And here was a water-laid path of white gravel, pummeled and sandy remains of rock. Lying flat, all prone on the floor of the valley of Wight Brook, the waster.

Wight the brook. Shall I say you are a noun of Anglo-Saxon origin? Or are you an adjective derived from the Old Norse? Do descendents of the old settler named Wight, who may still live in this valley, know which it is?

Coming to Maine in Winter

It's second shift, Allen is working, the sun has just gone down. Outside this house—our Massachusetts landlord's house—the wind is squalling, but, as I listen, it sounds less thunderous than in hours past. I've been thinking of walking up the hill. Our thermometer says high 30s but the wind will whip body heat off rapidly. I spy Allen's quilt-lined coat hanging on its peg, decide to wear it, and make the walk.

I'm out into the wind and over to that tree where the dog, Boots, is chained. Lying forlorn in a leaf-filled depression, he's getting used to being chained since the incident with the animal control officer (euphemism). He's not tearing up the ground much anymore. He rises and comes to me, patient. I stoop to unhook him and he's off in this wind like a projectile. He looks hastily over his shoulder to see what direction I want, then leaps up the road. He'd better look: He's hard of hearing.

I follow. The dog's joy in release is infectious. As he looks, I clap my mittened hands and he darts ahead.

Walking rapidly, I look around, turn in a circle, barely breaking my stride. There is the horizon of dark ridges and hills through tall spindly trees. Their edges are glowing with a last lick of light. I turn again to walk uphill backward, feeling the difference in muscle tension in the backs of my legs. I tilt my head to see into treetops, naked and fine-branched, blowing like wands in the wind.

My pace tries to match that of the wind, but as I pass a dark thick section of woods, I'm stopped still by a weird whistling in those trees. I peer through waving darkness. The piercing noise stops, resumes, stops. I cannot see the source but decide it's one of those creatures—a noise made in treetops by squealing branches rubbing against one another. It seems I find this more often in winter . . . or do I just notice it more?

Reaching the top of the first flat, I notice again a great barn-or-mansion-sized house being finished on my old lookout spot. Last winter I stood on that bare lot and peered out across the valley when visibility was good—across eight folds of the hills into the White Mountains, the "Big Boys," as some friends have dubbed them, *The Presidentials.* Now, passing some parked vehicles of workers, I gawk at the great u-shaped structure, two massive wings of which stare at each other across a small court. The wind tears at its plastic covers blowing in shreds across elongated windows. My looking is so intent that I turn only just in time to keep from ramming myself into a pickup with projecting metal framework.

I skirt the truck, glad no one's around to witness my folly but the dog. Or is there? A dark shape moves in the passenger seat; a younger woman who turns and rolls down the window.

Feeling foolish I blurt, "Wasn't watching my step and I almost walked into your truck." Assuming that others notice my gaffes I'm always quick to point them out myself.

"I'm sorry." The friendly face with hair pulled back in a ponytail was apologizing.

"Do you think this is a doctor's office or something?" I'm asking because the place is so big it's a wonder if some professional will be doing such business out of his or her home.

We discuss the property in question, then she admires my dog. He seems a good dog . . . and I affirm that indeed he is.

She says her husband is inside, looking for work as a mason. I give the name of a mason who sometimes hires. She thanks me, and the dog and I go our way, considering.

I don't know what Boots is considering: perhaps squirrels. I'm thinking about a young couple, new in the area, perhaps new to Maine, near the end of November, looking for work. And I'm thinking about another couple in their mid-thirties, with two sons approaching adolescence, also new in Maine, the husband looking for work . . . on the brink of winter.

That second, almost middle-aged couple, broke down on the main street of Freeport, a block from L.L. Bean's. Their used 12-year-old ex-luxury car needed a push to the nearest garage, and there was less than $90 in the woman's purse. That was seven years ago now.

I know that young pony-tailed woman sitting in the car, waiting for her husband while he makes the rounds looking for work in a strange new place. I know her because she is close to being that *me* of seven years ago. As I walk on, now staring across-valley at the spotted lights of the hamlet, I think strong thoughts for another newcomer: *Welcome to Maine. May it do for you all it has done for us, and more.*

The dog and I walk a little further then turn back. Arriving again past the great gray structure I notice the pickup is gone. Someone in a stocking cap approaches another truck from the house. One of the workmen, no doubt. The truck has four, maybe five, screened cubbyholes in a hutch above its bed.

I call out: "Do you carry sled dogs in your truck?"

The answer is affirmative, in the voice of a young woman. She's a carpenter working temporarily on the house.

"Do you run sled dogs, then? I'm looking for someone who runs dogs. It might be nice to write about the sport—in a creative way," I add this hastily, hoping to raise no false hopes about seeing something in print. "I don't particularly write for any magazine."

"You're doing a book?"

I admit as much. Actually, I'm doing four books, but no one is yet doing the publishing. However I say nothing of this. I write on faith, Allen finds work on faith, we drive 12-year-old cars with almost no money to strange places where you have to look hard for employment—on faith. The dog stays tied up behind at a friend's and contemplates squirrels for over a year, on faith, until we have enough money to return to Pennsylvania for him and some few of our broken down possessions. We always make sure to do this sort of thing on the brink of winter with two almost adolescents in tow. Maybe *I* am a book. If not, I'm at least a good story.

She hands me her card and explains that she hires out dog sled rides, dog packing for shoers in the winter, and she is a guide. In summer she and her husband, who is also a registered guide, provide wilderness canoeing and climbing trips. He's an ice climber. It's too dark to see the card now, but later I'll find out, their fledgling business is Mahoosuc Mountain Adventures.

I'm excited and my questions come quickly, not very coherent. I've just been given a present in the form of a stocking cap and a pickup truck with sled-dog cubbyholes.

The present rolls off downhill, leaving the dog and me to make our way down to the lighted house.

On our way, I'm arrested suddenly by a screech from the woods above a wall of grim dim granite. I look up, into black clumps of evergreens, noting again the winter squeaker. The woods are full of strange noises and surprises, especially at night, near the end of November.

Godly Little Birds

Allen and I drive down to town for winter errands. Fifty degrees and the 3rd of December, a continuing mild autumn with a few Indian Summers. A scum of ice tries forming on ponds, sending crystals far-reaching, only to thaw next day. We have delicate ice on the surface of the north pond in our town.

We took Outlaw Valley Road and stopped at a small greenhouse cum floral establishment by the road. Wreaths were fixed to the side of the shed/barn, simple evergreens with red bows and pine cones, swags with colored ribbons and cones. Seven dollars, or ten for the larger. But I was also after a bird with nest. I had called around a little and could find no birds, no nests. I wanted them for a wreath I was hoping to compose for my mother-in-law.

I dreamed she was standing on tiptoe looking at a wreath on the back of our house, saying, "Oh look, here's a little bird."

It would make a lovely present, but I was finding artificial birds with real nests scarce.

Allen waited for me in the car as I walked around back and found the door. I looked through its pane and saw a feminine figure at work in the little room, put my hand on the brass knob, pushed open the door.

"Do you have any little birds and nests?" The young woman looked back at me out of the shiny panes perched on her nose—outsized glasses. She seemed nonplussed by my request, went rummaging through boxes; and found a bedraggled cardinal but would not consider him. He stayed in the beribboned clutter while she went for another box. I looked at him carefully, picked him up. No he would not do. Not with his deep red harsh contours, but I was so glad that someone had a bird I was willing to consider him.

Then she thrust a box beneath my eyes and delicate subtle colors came up at me: the dainty forms of speckled birds wrapped in clear cellophane. Real *birdness* in a box.

Slowly I reached inside and picked one up. It weighed nothing and looked at me vulnerably with one eye. The eye was in a pointed head of burnished feathers before a speckled back. Its wing feathers were golden. Its tiny claws clasped some twigs. It was the real thing as pretend birds go. Remove the cellophane and it might fly away.

I was enchanted, could hardly speak, but managed to ask, "How much?"

"A dollar fifty."

A dollar fifty! For an enchanted almost living bird looking at me with one eye? The eye on the opposite side of its tiny pointed face could be seen by turning the bird on its twigs, but when I did this that eye looked away, as though we could meet visually only from its left side.

That this bird, this enchantment, would cost only $1.50 as though two sparrows could be bought for a penny. If gold were to come alive . . . if gold were alive it might be a bird breathing fiercely, containing a metabolism necessary for flight.

This young woman, who possessed the ability to have birds wrapped in cellophane appear from a box, had no bird's nests. She told me how to make one myself out of Spanish moss.

My crest drooped. How could I go to north Florida on such short notice to gather Spanish moss for my mother-in-law's bird nest?

"You can get it," she was saying, "down at Woolworth's in South Paris."

Allen pulls into the parking space at Ames, and, because the radio is on, leaves the key in the ignition. He goes off to get antifreeze. I am listening intently to a quartet of flutes on *St. Paul Sunday Morning* because I need inspiration for the faerie romance I'm working on, lately, at my desk. The melodious scale being offered is like a polychrome tonal scale from bass clarinet to piccolo. Ah.

Allen returns and we start for the other end of town, me surreptitiously looking for Christmas trees, Christmas tree prices. For some ungodly reason, people in our household don't seem interested in Christmas. Is it ungodly to grow up? My sons are college-aged adults. My husband needs children under his feet in order to feel the excitement of the season. It would help if the temperature fell 20° with snow gently falling. Fifty degrees in early December around here might also be ungodly.

"Oh, look," I commented innocently as we passed a truck flanked and obscured by evergreens. "Only six dollars and up."

Allen kept driving. We drove on to the other side of town, and by this time I had him talked up to a tree. We pulled into a lot where they stood on display: $29.95 read one tag. He turned the car around and headed in the direction from which we had come.

We pulled into the dirt lot where the tree-crammed truck stood. Off to one side I saw a boy building a mud castle, patting it with his hands. As he worked he called to the young man who stood indifferently by the truck full of evergreens. "Yeah yeah," he said dismissively to the boy.

I walked around the truck, surveying those goods of the forests, some large, and in some cases quite spindly. The young man followed, his hands rammed into his pockets, not particularly interested in pulling out trees for my perusal.

An airplane droned overhead and the boy looked up from his work, shouting.

The young man said, out of a square-jawed face scarred with acne, "Yeah yeah. It's only an airplane."

It must be ungodly to grow up.

"How much?" I pulled out the spindling, smallest of the lot.

"Eight dollars. They're expensive, but my uncle sets the price and he's not here."

But the sign says six dollars. I say nothing, continue walking around the trees. I get back into the car without speaking and we pull out, leaving the little castle-building boy behind. But he stays in my thoughts.

We drive back to town, Allen looking for a place to get coffee; self looking for trees. He spies the coffee shop, I spy trees in a parking lot, and we agree to park halfway between. I'm to meet him for hot coffee after I check out the trees.

I approach the lot. Another truck with trees. Trees also propped along the perimeter of the lot, strewn along a driveway below, down toward a trailer where many more are stacked like cordwood.

An old man, with entirely puckered face and hearing aid visible in his left ear, tells me the difference in price between plantation and wild trees. He has a few of the latter. His helper, a black-haired Native American followed his instruction, accompanying me and we came down to the wild trees.

"Would you hold this one up for me?" He brought it out from among the others and held it up for my measuring gaze: short, spindly at the tiptop, bushy everywhere else. I *could* put it on a stand.

We looked at every tree, eyeballing them, some he handled at my request. His eyes were coal black like his hair, he an adolescent, helpful and pleasant. Not the boy of the castles, nor the cynical youth with acne performing a hateful chore for his uncle.

At last we came back to the first tree, the wild tree. The puckered man came over and, at his invitation, we haggled. The price was settled, I handed him a $10 bill and the youth shouldered the prickly tree. We headed for the car, still parked halfway between the coffee shop and Christmas trees.

"Is that your grandfather?" We walked together, the boy with tree and I.

"He's my uncle."

Ah.

"Do you live around here?"

"We live in Hebron. Not far."

We approach the car and I open the hatch. He asked how I wanted the tree placed. When the hatch was closed I hand him a small amount in today's currency, but he seemed glad of it. I was glad of him.

We separated, he going toward the convenience store nearby. I went to the coffee shop to see Allen and drink coffee. I had two uncles, two nephews, godly little birds, and a castle in my thoughts.

Dave's Sauna

After buying wreaths, trees and coffee, we drove over to Dave's Sauna, the sauna sprawling beside the Little Androscoggin River. It's a cedar shake and quasi stucco building with bedraggled dusty ferns hanging in its dirty picture windows. The lot is heaped with piles of mill ends that Dave uses to fire the stoves in his private saunas.

Lately, when I think of Dave, I think of wood. He has woods, sells wood, handles wood. Not just mill ends, but whole forests of wood. The land beside his farmhouse, located on the main road between our town and

South Paris, is piled tens of feet high with logs for firewood. His land is rich with raw logs.

During the back-to-the-land movement, Dave bought the sauna by mortgaging his first Maine property, bought with bar mitzvah gifts. His customers were (and still are, largely) Finns, fellow back-to-the-landers, and old hippies like Allen and I. Skiers and hunters enjoy the sauna, too.

Allen pushes open the glass door for me and we enter, walk past a cluttered picnic table toward the counter, where he shells out seven dollars. Bearded Dave, standing behind it, asks if we need anything—soap, towels? But we brought our overnight bag along with shampoo and a fresh change of clothes. His son is readying a room for us, so we stand and make small talk for a minute or two. I didn't know Dave had a son old enough to help in the sauna. I guess the years do pass. It's our first visit of the new decade, last of the millennium. The bespeckled adolescent, now Hebrew man, emerges from the hallway, finished with disinfectant mopping, and we go down the dimly lighted corridor to dressing-room number six.

The sauna is nothing but funky. It is paneled and smoke-dark and knotty pine. The locks are rusted and largely inoperable; doubled with hooks-and-eyes. Each hot-room has two attached dressing rooms floored in yellowing knotty pine. The disinfectant keeps it light-colored, bleached.

We undress in the private inner room and enter the small sauna room naked. I dump soap and wash rags on the lower bench and step up to lock the door of that dressing room next to ours.

Allen is already seated on the top bench against a knotty pine wall. The top bench is hottest because of rising heated air. I climb up and join him, but at the opposite end.

I'm thinking of writing about Dave's sauna, so instead of relaxing completely, I look carefully at my surroundings: The cubicle appears to be about 8 x 8 with one wall and the chimney of cement block. The other walls are pine, very dark, almost black, with initials and names carved into them. Bleached benches, white plastic bucket containing white mill ends: yet our two winter-white bodies stick out visually in the dank, gloomy atmosphere. That atmosphere is made drearier by one glaring yellow bulb hanging from a ceiling socket.

The sauna stove is made of thin steel. It has a trough on one side, full of water. Stones are piled in a niche atop the stove beside its stovepipe. The description wouldn't be complete without a key component to this atmosphere: water in two of its physical forms, liquid and vapor. Here are pipes

3/4 inches in diameter traveling along the warped pine ceiling. Condensed water drips from a cold water pipe with a chilling effect on anyone happening below. The showers offer hot and cold. Galvanized buckets and dipper are standing nearby. The air is steamy and stifling.

The sauna is ugly and confining.

But, *ohhh . . .*

I stretch out on the bench, close my eyes and soak in it. Never was ugliness so relaxing. The heat, the steam pulling and pummeling my skin and pores, draining away the week's tension spent hunched over a typewriter, eyes tensely moving along thousands of lines of typescript. A week of doing nothing but adhering to that one position in that one room. Gone.

Gone out in steam and heat. My body is slick with sweat, the sweat it would've yielded had I the equivalent labor in Allen's physical job.

I'm no longer in an ugly, dripping, stifling room. I'm anywhere my mind can find its rest with accompanying mental images. Then—unexpectedly—the pleasure of the soapy hands of my lover massaging my calves.

I think no one ever put their coming-of-age to better use: a 13-year-old youth put his bar mitzvah gifts into investments which ended decades later in this pleasurable experience for uncounted winter-weary Mainers.

Our hour ends all too soon. I unlock the next-door dressing room. We enter our own room and dry off. Allen peeked out the hallway door and called out number six. As I dressed I heard Dave's son come down the hall and into the room next door. He went into the hot room and began mopping up.

We stopped on our way out to say goodbye. Dave was talking to an old Mainer when I asked how big the rooms were. He looked at the old Mainer. "How big?" He explained that this was the man who originally built and operated the business before him—when it was Dick's Sauna.

"The charge back then?" I asked.

"A dollar. I tried to raise it to a dollar and quarter but they hollered."

We hadn't been to the sauna since the winter before, but were customers off and on, five or six years. When we came out of the corridor, Dave would always ask "How was it?"

He didn't do that this time.

On my way out, I noticed his son sitting on the dilapidated couch against the wall. I gestured toward him pointedly with my hairbrush: "Thank you."

The youth asked, "How was it?"

"Beautiful." I smiled.

Green Black White

12–16-90, at the window/desk. Finished Micah; read Christ's sermon on the mount. Indexed five pages of Washburn-Norlands' Journals. Washed bathroom fixtures. Boxed and wrapped my mother-in-law's wreath. Typing chapter three.

Outside a squirrel scampers out, digs beneath cakey snow for a pine cone. Turning it round and round, the squirrel dismantles this cone with its teeth, row by row rapidly, as befits its metabolism. It hops up on a snow-caked rock, continues dismantling its cone, littering the snow with scales. It jumps down, scampers to a spindly trees stump, perches there, eating cone seeds, looking about.

Yesterday was the first day of atmospheric (not calendar) winter for this season. I walked through stiff snow, unhooked the dog and together we walked uphill through a stinging wind. The sky all round was pastel cold: cold pale pinks, vivid blues, and varying whites; the grays of late sunset afternoons. Fresh, strong, with a peculiar combination of pale and vivid winter sky hurrying against somber forest green and steel-gray hills fringed with pointed firs.

The wind brushed up the dog's black fur.

As I walked, slightly bent into the hill and the north, I plotted fictional chapter titles, synopses, alternating between concentrated thought and grateful awareness of all my surroundings. Often I turned and walked backward up this hill, needing to see a part of that sky where the sun had gone. Needing respite from the breath of the north. Floating cloud-color permeated all sections of sky except in direst north.

As I gulped strong air and turned this way and that I thought of writing some words—"It is winter and my breath is taken away." Words to say, yes, I remember now. *Winter*. It comes yearly when the North drops down to take a bite. It is winter and the north is here with fierce cold breath.

12–16-90, same day.

    Things to ask Polly Mahoney

    What interested you about dog-sled racing?

    How'd you get started? Training?

    Do you teach it?

    Background she originates from?

    How do you race dogs?

    How do I get to your place?

    What's your job on Deer Hill?

12–17-90, Saturday.

Breakfast at the Colonial in Norway. They have decent sausages this time. Look at some snow tires at VIP. Made copies of stories to submit to magazines in Lewiston, in Portland. Groceries.

    Just talked to Polly—to call again at noon

    Meet at her place 9:30 a.m. tomorrow—Boston teenagers (Outward Bound)

    (Hired as carpenter—sheet rocking drywall mudding & taping—Polly's work at the big u-shaped house.)

Monday on 12–11-90

    Writing yesterday's meeting of Polly Mahoney at her house in North Newry.

    Notes from today. Breakfast the Red Top. Go with Allen to Lewiston for doctor's appointment and his eye exam. Got historical documents of Grandpa's missions over Germany and France laminated for the boys and Allen. Saw "Blue Runways" in Portland Monthly Magazine in a store in

Lewiston. Don't like the title change. And he labeled it fiction!! I drive home because Allen's got drops in his eyes.

Polly Mahoney lives seven or eight miles up a desolate highway, seemingly on the way to nowhere. A Maine designated scenic highway which I've written about before . . . in the opening pages of *Maine Metaphor*, and even in the pages of this particular winter journal when I wrote about the landslide and Step Falls.

One arrives at the sprawling connected dwelling with attached red barn, sensing the old, cold, barren winter of a bygone time. One looks at the house and thinks, "It can't possibly be warm in there." It's on the edge of the Notch, south of Wight Brook, where immigrants, broke and disconsolate, feared and abandoned.

But then I enter and find all that light. Light from the gift of windows, and warm with an invisible (to me) heat source. A large sprawling house can have more and higher windows to send light everywhere over its white walls and warm woodwork, the semi-bare floor, the brick fireplace (unlit). It is Sunday and this house is lit by sun and by snow. We finally had our long-awaited snow. Now we can get on with our winter.

Marginalia: Yukon—job, isolated. Fish meal.

Polly Mahoney is trim, 31 years old, honey-blonde, and modest. Her gentleness and slight frame belie the inner toughness of a dogsled musher who lived an isolated Yukon life for 10 years. Looking past her I see on her bookshelves the titles of *Jack London: Stories of Adventure*, *Arctic Dreams*, *Of Wolves and Men*, and *Land Above the Trees*, among other similar titles.

I'm here to learn a little about dog sledding, and Polly, as one half of Mahoosuc Mountains Adventures, is going to teach me some things. Husband Kevin Slater is the other half. She leads me out into a connecting shed where gear and dog food are kept. Talking about the nutritional and physical elements of the sled dog diet, she dumps a scant amount of dog food into two white plastic buckets; sprinkling this with fish meal and handing me a metal pot, asking if I want to fetch hot water for the food.

With this act, one can tell that Polly is indeed a teacher. She teaches, among other things, how to survive in the wilderness. Get the student participating, if only to fetch water. Sunlight, oxygen, and water, complements in maintaining material physical existence. If she doesn't flavor it with food and fish meal (a powder of dried fish, fish bones, and offal, dogs will not drink enough water and will stop to eat snow instead. The real meal comes later, at night. I turn the spigot for hot water, and dump it into the food-water plastic buckets. She puts chicken fat on a stick then dunks it into the warm water, stirring.

Now we are ready for the other students. They appear, as if on cue, outside the big house. The cobalt blue van with white lettering on its rear door announces: *Outward Bound, Thompson Island, Boston Massachusetts.*

City kids. The program's motto is personal growth through outdoor adventure.

Fetching hats and mittens from the car, I do a double-take as I see that the half-dozen plus male students are mostly black. As a kid I went to church in my father's old neighborhood in a Midwestern city, a neighborhood of what we then called the colored people. The yards of houses, where dark children played, were black with packed earth. It was always a wonder to drive by and see those yards where not one blade of grass grew. My own yard, the yard of my green childhood, was fringed and cool. For blocks around, for miles, there was a green patchwork of fair yards and lawns. And there were no black bodies squatting over marbles, no brown arms swinging bats, no scraped shins bloody and dark.

Some of my forebears were part of the great Appalachian migration from the slopes of West Virginia who, like some African-Americans of that day, had come north to the land of steel and rubber industries for a better life. One branch of the family had been so poor they went barefoot even in winter. In the city my white antecedents had been able to work hard and make a good life for their children. Their yards became green. But they left the neighborhood to African-Americans who had been unable to keep them green. Based on this indelible impression of childhood, the color of reparation is green. The yard of injustice is darkened and compacted in our America.

Who knows how long until there's a black mayor of Boston? It will be 20 years before Massachusetts has a black governor. Twenty years for that African-American president. These teenage young men will be middle-aged. So, since coming to white yankee Anglo-Saxon Maine, I've always done a double-take upon seeing African-Americans here, so rare is their presence in this rough rural landscape.

That impression wears off and they aren't so much dark skinned as they are teenagers. Already they're griping about being here in this desolate place, in this barren cold, about to meet up with dogs. Despite this carping, they're game. Two of Polly's dogs are fenced out here by the drive and the boys approach, some with trepidation, others with eagerness. All are varying degrees of wary at first.

"OK," says one, "I've seen them now let's get out of here."

"Yo. Roll over," says another to the great wolfish part-Huskies.

One of the dogs begins to bark and a third teenager says, "I'm not gonna take that kind of abuse."

After a short conversation with the Outward Bound teachers, Polly comes by and leads us around the fencing and connected red barn, to the back of the house—behind the shed where the food/water waits in buckets. There my attention escapes as I see a magnificent desolation spread out before me, white snowfield, the distant tree-bristling ridge. Mountains hunkering over them, clouds moving above on the winter breeze. All is fresh and pure, swift and keen. And I hear the desolation. I hear it in wind, distant throats of dogs, chained and fenced in woods far below hulking wilderness mountains.

I don't believe, oh no! I don't believe in the narrow and somewhat pedantic definition of wilderness abroad these days. We have scant genuine wilderness, the purists say. I'm glad they say it, that they call it into our beleaguered attention. But I believe wilderness is any place possessed of the power to bewilder. Being a mile away from this spot, up there in those old steep hills, with only what I know now about wilderness survival and navigation—that would truly bewilder me. It would surely bewilder these city teenagers. By like token, I would be and have been bewildered walking along Boston's fore and back streets, feeling vulnerable about my lack of money or credit cards. But I don't think I would've been desolate. People—sitting, walking, riding—keep desolation at bay.

Polly Mahoney's backyard desolation is a reviving draft. I stand in it rapt for an age. I could stay a day contemplating. I would lie down in it the night long. And I could willingly die in it. I will be dying someday.

Do I just dream wilderness dying is preferable?

Polly stands talking amid a semicircle of a few Outward Bound staff members and these city youths, all decked in winter garb, with boots brought by truck specially for the occasion. Boots supplant sneakers for dog sledding. Polly explains what the students will be doing once we've crossed the snow-covered field and reached the fenced dogs. She takes off her stocking cap, stuffs in a few bits of paper and holds out the cap, urging each student to pick a dog's name. Some of the staff pick names as well. Polly says there's one left and holds out the hat to me.

We each have a dog to pet, to feed, possibly to harness to the sled, and to scoop poop for.

"Do what?" asks one boy in disbelief, several echoing his attitude.

The name on my slip reads Kipmik, a Native American or Inuit sounding name. I think of kinnikinnick, the only such word I know. Something to smoke, I think.

Straggling a multicolored queue across snowy fields into woods, we approach the fenced, exuberant, barking mixed huskies. Next to a stream of black waters sits a tarp-covered four-wheeler, an uncovered four-wheeler sans engine—and the, to my eyes, mythic-looking dog sled. (It does occur to me that in an earlier age the four-wheelers would be mythic looking . . . not the dog sleds.)

Though roughly triangular in profile, it has a canvas sling lashed to a frame of metal and wood with runners extending rearward. Just above these runners is a metal foot brake. I ask Polly if the brake works well against hyper-straining dog flesh.

"It does on packed snow, but not on fresh powder." She then points out that she's hooking the sled to a stake behind it—to keep the dogs from running off with the sled before she's got every last one in its traces.

We turn to the straining barkers inside fenced pens, two pens. One for puppies and one for trained and seasoned haulers.

I enter the puppy pen because that's where Kipmik is chained beside her hutch. The snow in this pen is packed down around each of the half-dozen stakes where these mixed huskies tug and jump. Polly has assured everyone that the dogs are just glad to see us and won't bite, but instinctive wariness persists in some of the city kids. They approach their dogs timidly.

Kipmik, whose name means Arctic Fox, is a beautiful all white part-Samoan. Other dogs are mixed huskies with part Siberian or part Alaskan malamute mixed in. None are purebred and the lead dog, Hermes, is only 1/8 wolf. I pet Kipmik, trying to make friends with the five-month-old but it's no use—she's already friendly and just glad to have some attention.

Polly's method of training the pups is to let them follow behind the team as she mushes: this, until they are six months old when patient training begins in earnest. Polly instructs the students—whose dogs are team members—how to bring them to the sled. The part-huskies are so excited and anxious to be in their traces that they need to be brought to it with special handling. Making dogs easier to control, front legs must be lifted off the ground: coming on two feet only. Five students each bring a dog thusly, first lifting it by the collar until its front feet are in the air. They come willingly . . . but they are odd-looking—prancers.

Polly is showing how they are fitted in their traces and now each student, with the help of a staff person, gets his dog harnessed and fitted up. One student is ready to ride, seated in the sling. These dogs are tense, awaiting the command. Polly unhooks the sled from its post, jumps on the runners and gives command. "Let's go!" They're gone, tearing across the snow.

Around leafless thicket of alders, along the edges of woods. I rush through thick crusty stuff for a better view and see them disappear into the trees. I've lost sight. Now I see them again, coming unexpectedly back through trees only to disappear and emerge beyond the pens and continue around and back toward the waiting group. Now I hurry along to witness a rider's response to his first sled-dog ride.

Jimmy climbs out of the sling, quiet but smiling. I study his soft black eyes and ask him if he liked it, though it's evident in his look. It was a mistake, my trying to urge him to speak by saying I am a writer. This produces no change in his unhurried manner. Then I say the one thing I've always despised in an interview: I ask how he *feels* about the ride—true indicator of a questioner's inability to evoke a "feeling" response. But finally he says "I thought we were going to crash, especially there," pointing toward a sharp crook in the trail.

Everyone gets a turn, some riding on a back runner beside Polly, yelling verbal commands. The words "Let's go," must be used in place of the traditional "mush". . . but it seems to take *any* tone of command. When the dogs become distracted while awaiting the next rider, Polly says "Hermes, tighten up," and they all respond by falling into line and, in fact, tightening up. When a student tells a dog to sit, Polly says, as if that sort of command were beneath them, "They don't sit." I ask her how they learn the commands and she says through repetition. I visualize five untrained pups tangled in traces and don't envy her the job. It must take much patience.

One student, wearing two gold earrings in one ear, says, "If I could come down here every time I was in Maine, that'd be all right." Polly encourages this with a brief description of the fun of traveling all day and camping at night.

When rides are over, Polly tells the kids to take the dogs off their traces and unharness them; to bring them back to the pens two-legged, as before. "Pat the dogs and thank them for the ride." The kids have loosened up considerably. They hold bowls out to Polly for her to ladle the dog gruel into them. Each carries gruel to his dog.

Jimmy, watching Pan wolf hers, says, "Pan is a wild dog." He looks at another and says that Lena is calm. Lena is the oldest," says Polly, "even older than Hermes."

I go to the pups' pen to feed Kipmik. Polly comes to ladle gruel. I set the bowl on packed snow before this frisking dog and she begins lapping it. The gruel on my hands is greasy. I spend the rest of the visit occasionally trying to get it off my palms and fingers with snow. Pick up the shovel and bucket by the particleboard gate and go around Kipmik's yard, scooping the poop. Take the bucketful along a packed trail past the pen. Looking down on a pile of frozen shit, among thickets I wonder if it will ever compost.

Polly asks, "Do you want to roughhouse with the pups?" and gets an enthusiastic response. The pups are unchained and tear out of the fence to race with one another and play among the students.

Pups gang up on Kipmik, the only all-white dog, biting his neck. "Are they are showing dominance?" I ask. She replies that usually Kipmik acts dominant but for some reason today the reverse is so. The black teenagers joke about that. One says "Whitey's finally getting it back." This brings a roar of laughter. Then Polly asks for Bridey, the pups' mother, to be loose among them and out she comes to roughhouse with them.

I notice that one of the pups, Sheena, has blood on her fur, her ruff and back. Polly, overhearing me mention this to one of the staff, says it happens. Bridey chases one pup like-size with herself, and wrestles it to the ground repeatedly. It crouches submissively until it thinks her attention has wandered. Then it tears off, but Bridey is again after it. "It's the cockiest pup in the litter and she wants to restrain this tendency."

Off to one side a group of kids have begun a snowball fight, aiming all at one in particular. The Boston Outward Bound staffer, to whom I pointed out the blood, says, "Those guys are like the pups. See how they pick and gang up on him?"

It's time to put Bridey and the pups back and then head for home. After the gates are closed and we start back to the house, I ask gold earrings if he has found a career here. "I like the dogs, yeah; but not the cold. Definitely not the cold." Again our multihued queue straggles back across the field.

The surrounding mountains—forested, dark and white—distract my attention from the group. My gaze leaps out northward to the massive cloud spread with great weight across a blue sky. My gaze leaps again toward the heft and imponderable wild of the mountain. I do a double-take: There is a great white scar down its desolate dark flank. The scar, made by the landslide not long ago, is livid, harsh. In the distance the dogs behind us are howling.

"Hear that?" Polly says to anyone. "They don't want us to leave. They're saying *Come back, come back.*"

I hear them.

Resonant, echoing, lonesome and wild.

Hermes Knows

I rose at five to make coffee, breakfast and lunch. We rode to the mill town twenty miles away. I dropped Allen off to use the car. I had a date with dogs.

I pulled out onto the dirty winter highway and took off. My mind was racing, fueled by McD's coffee. Time to slow the car, take my time. I didn't want to get to Polly's, in Grafton Notch, before our appointment at 10 a.m. I drove on, listening to a morning duo on the oldies station, but I was thinking of a narrative waiting for me at home. Every few tenths of a mile something would occur to me. I'd pull over onto the shoulder beside a dirty snow pile to write it down. I was beginning to shape the character of our heroine and everything pertaining must not be allowed to escape. She was to embody poetry. I pulled the car over on a gravel shoulder off the highway and wrote that on an envelope found in my purse. Once, as I pulled back onto the highway, I looked over my shoulder for traffic and saw a hilltop in burnished splendor reflecting golden rays of early sun, rays shot from beneath gray clouds in the east.

At last, driving ten miles under the speed limit, I come to a lonely spot where the highway turns north and runs many miles showing little but winter desolation and greatly moving beauty all the way to Quebec, Canada. I come to Polly's rambling federalist house, but go past, driving into the Notch to feel its dark lonesome hills shouldering up around me, see rushing waters of Screw Auger Falls pouring out of many mountains. Then I turn round and head back toward Polly's in timely fashion.

Polly was raised rurally—hills and lakes, no mountains—in South China, Maine; attending Augusta schools in the state capital. When she was twenty she went to work for the Park Service in Alaska. Alaska, I sometimes think, is full of young Mainers. Those who love the wild beauty of Maine are often tempted by the wilder bigger beauty of Alaska.

Polly learned to mush from her ex-husband while in the Yukon. She also bred dogs there. Dogs were used to maintain life, used in fetching firewood and supplies, in providing needed exercise for the musher. Mushing is hard work, I was soon to learn. In Maine she uses her dogs for recreation and teaching, and also commercially in guiding and packing into the backcountry. She enjoys sharing her experience with those familiar and unfamiliar with dog sledding.

However, being here, where it's far less rugged, wild, and isolated, means a slightly altered relationship with the dogs . . . and the life. Polly says she's not now as attuned to the dogs as she was in the Yukon. She's no longer as land-and-dog connected as when isolated circumstance forced on her a larger inner life. In order to escape isolation, she returned to Maine. Now Polly and her husband-partner Kevin Slater can go contra-dancing in Gray or do business in Portland if they want to. And up here there is work doing what she loves.

We come out to get sled dogs ready for this morning's work. The puppies are to be harnessed for their first time and made to run as part of a team. They are used to chasing behind veteran teams, but today they'll be tried out in the traces. Polly hands me the lead line and I string it out in front on crusty snow, hooking to the stake, then straighten up the neck- and tug-lines so they can be hooked to dogs in harness.

Polly says we'll try two inexperienced pups with three veterans. We enter the pen of experienced dogs and I unhook dark Lena and bring her out, careful to lift her off her front paws by the collar, and lead her two-legged. I try to get this part-husky into the harness, but have forgotten the technique. Polly refreshes my memory by reminding me to grasp Lena's rear between my knees. Lena is patient and submissive in handling. I give her a pat by way of thanks after hooking her collar to neck-line, the end of her harness to tug line.

Polly hooks Hermes in lead position. He is the veteran lead. Hermes was in the movie *Never Cry Wolf*, in the lead dog position of Ootek, part of the shaman's team. And Polly was the stunt-double musher for that sha-man. A movie with mythic tones strong enough to captivate imaginations for its premise of beleaguered nature. Hermes is finally tuned to four com-mands: *Let's go* (for mush), *gee*, *haw*, and *whoa*. There are no reins except the voice. And Hermes is firmly attached to it. When he hears *tighten up* he stops goofing off and stands ready in his *let's go* position.

I go get Kipmik, the all white pup. She will get her first taste of har-nessed running, excited and unused to being uplifted by her collar and made to prance over packed snow on two feet. When I try to harness her she ends on the ground in a submissive heap, uneasy over this strange treat-ment at the hands of a stranger.

Polly notices and quickly comes to rescue us, deciding to harness the pups their first time—that their initial experiences might be pleasant and assuring. This—plus the fact that I have harnessed Kipmik in such a tangled fashion . . . the harness lying along Kipmik's white belly instead of her back!

Kipmik is placed on the left beside Lena. A white and black paring of wheel dogs, those closest to sled and musher. Out comes Kango, another pup—placed beside Bridey, his mother, in swing position right behind Hermes.

All are hooked in their traces and Hermes tightens up. Polly tells me how to place my feet, one behind the other on the runner. I grab the frame with mittened hands.

"Let's go!" We are off over crusty snow on a track already laid. I watch the dogs career through snow. The track is eroded from last night's rain, but a hard freeze has given this snow an edge.

The two pups, Kipmik left wheel dog, and Kango right swing dog, seem out of place and a bit bewildered running in traces. Kango, especially, looks back nervously at the sound of Polly's encouraging voice. As though it comes from the wrong direction. The voice should be in front, going on before, with Kango following in rapturous joy.—What he's used to.

One small part of me notices this as we zip and sway over snow. The larger part of me is simply trying to hang on, the part trying to avoid getting brushed across my eyes by alder twigs rushing past. I feel strange combination of working in concert while out of place. I see it in Kango's worried run. It's the old frantic what-the-heck-am-I doing here feeling. I try copying Polly's sled gait, kicking off with one foot to lighten the pulling of these dogs. My efforts are jerky, more a hindrance than help. Raising her voice a little, she advises me to swing my leg forward, after pushing back, give the kick a more fluid motion.

We enter woods and suddenly she warns of a coming turn. "Haw, Hermes." Wondrous sight: I see the redoubtable dark Hermes turn left and keep going. My admiration leaps after him. They move as one. Even the pups—while awkward and clearly worried—move well in concert on the turn. I feel a sense of easy intelligence come back to me from Hermes, Hermes the Greek god, presiding over roads and messengers. Here, on this snow among sudden trees, Hermes is wiser than I am. This fleeting arrangement of lines and straps and hooks and runners; flesh and fur. Hermes knows more than I do.

Comes a series of quick curves and a slender slat bridge we practically jump. I can only hold on. Finally we are exiting the woods, rounding that bend of the dog pens, coming to full halt before them.

Kevin, bearded and wearing a stocking cap, is there, readying his team for pup-training. He calls out asking how we're doing and Polly says the pups aren't doing as well as she'd hoped. She turns to me. We agree they will run without me on the next turn around the woods. She makes a quick exchange among the puppies and off they go, leaving behind a grateful puppy-out-of-place.

I stand a still moment, spread my legs a little, hoping to find feet with a proper hold on the snowy earth. Gravity could take me down now. They are gone. Polly, unbeknownst to me till later, stops to shift the dogs around again during the ride. Meanwhile I gaze on. The clouds are a movement of gray and white with vague shifting blues weaving overhead. Out across the valley I see celestial rays, pillars of light at odd angles, standing down from the sky. I look up to mighty mountains close above the distant house. A wind, roaring down from there has captured my attention. Gladly see the coniferous heights. I turn my vision toward Kevin and his trainee moving in and out pens, readying dogs for training. I'm exhilarated by panoramic nature and human experience. Full of meaning, metaphor and high purpose. And I, though without skill and peculiar knowledge, am part of it. For the time being.

Polly pulls out of woods and around the pens. She halts beside me. Sheena has been moved into lead position beside Hermes, and Polly is praising her in quiet dedicated voice. She has a feeling Sheena would make a good lead dog because of her confidence. Polly says we will double back and meet Kevin in the woods. Then he will follow us for our run down towards an opening, the Notch. Once again I position my feet on the wide runner, preparing to hang on.

There is no grace or feel for what I'm doing. Polly is quick to say that I do well for my first time, but at one point, after a brush-by collision with a tree too close to the path, I bail, asking her to pick me up on her way back. By this time trainee is in the woods with us, following fairly close with his team. I stand among trees, watching them disappear, grateful to be off the runner. My breath is ragged and forced from unaccustomed exertions.

Then—suddenly—standing among strange trees is a pleasure. Their brown linear stems and uncounted multitudes of twigs deepen, gather in thickets on the opposite side of this white track. I stand thinking of my failings, making excuses for my poor physical condition. Excuses might be all lined up and delivered with an apology for Polly.

They race into view and I cross behind to jump on again. Off we go, with Kevin coming up behind. On the next hill, I'm falling away. The last downhill is tricky and I am yet too short of breath, nearing exhaustion. Polly suggests I ride in the canvas sling. I except, gratefully.

"Keep your arms inside. We'll be on the downhill and able to fly over the last stretch."

At first I think the ride will be more terrifying because, in being a mere passenger, I have no recourse for control. But my fears ease as we speed along, and I can rest truly. How good it feels.

The pace picks up. We go downhill and these dogs sense the nearness of pen and pans. Pans full of food and water, leavings of butchers from the next town. The field of view opens, full of ice particles as I breathe bits thrown up by eager canines on their way to food. I close my eyes against the particles.

Hermes is on his way. Knowing. Wise. He needs no help from me.

Working Christmas

4:45 a.m. make coffee, plug in a white-lit wreath, turn on the radio to the Mt. Washington station playing Christmas carols.

Marginalia: read Brault's French-Canadian heritage in New England for info on St. P. & P. and people, remember theme of despised and rejected. Here in Maine the French were once so treated in the established Yankee culture.

Our son has graciously agreed. I will go to this church alone.

Relate when I'm inside the church; interspersed with service. Something on the language—the need to retain it. Newcomers retained their agrarian small-town mores and language in mill towns of Maine. "Lose your language, lose your faith."

Mountains beginning to be silhouetted against predawn twilight. The mill is wreathed in billowing steam, and smoke, like any morning, but it's Christmas. The employee's parking lot is almost, but not quite, as full of cars as on any day. Having dropped Allen off, I pull out onto the road, then look back over my right shoulder at this mill, at its ridges and hills of logs and chips, the grim grimy monstrous structures, smokestacks of our providence. As usual. There he will be the working electrician, as usual. Except that it's Christmas.

All is as usual when I drop my husband at his place of work and move on down the highway. A Christmas difference seen on the highway itself: deserted for long stretches. The road to a Catholic/French papermill town is dry and cold. I drive fifteen miles until coming to a closed convenience store; pull up beside a roadside phone sitting next the parking lot. "Operator, can I make collect call?

"What's your number?"

Collegiate J.D. answers and says he will accept the call. I ask him to check if the stove is off, if the wreath is unplugged. The wreath, he tells me, is lit. I wish him a Merry Christmas, say a few friendly words, and bye: we won't spend much of it together today. We had a family exchange of gifts and dinner the night before, and he assured me it would be all right—his spending much of the sacred day at home alone.

How—? How can I be off away and him home alone?

I pull away in the Subaru and proceed 25 miles down-highway, carols tinkling on the radio. The roadside is dirty with old snow, gritty with sand, pocked by melting from salt. The sun is just beginning to fire the fir hills. Transforming them.

It is Christmas Day 1990. I arrive into Auburn down route 4, glide past empty parking lots and deserted stores of Center Street and down into the inner business district. Pull to a stop and wait for the traffic light to change. A young happy-looking man in a red windbreaker walks in front of the car . . . now looking like reaching for the passenger side door handle, so I stretch out a forefinger and press the lock, averting my gaze from his smiling face, ashamed. I suspect he's developmentally disabled and feel ungenerous for refusing to share even a smile with what could be an angel in disguise. Or was he drunk? Neither of my sons, I think, would have refused him. My hard suspicious nature has robbed me of a telling moment.

He passes away down Court Street toward Lewiston and the light changes; I turn that way myself. Cross the bridge above Androscoggin River to enter the old textile mill town. Stop to make another collect call on pretext of determining whether I unplugged the coffee pot before leaving earlier. During the exchange J.D. and I wish one another Merry Christmas again and I'm listening for a tone, a timber in his voice to determine if he's unhappy about being alone. His tone is light, uncomplicated, content. I hang up, and sigh.

Morning coffee has triggered the bladder and I'm in need of relief: but where can one find a public toilet in a deserted city French-Catholic city on Christmas Day?

I drive desultorily, vaguely hoping an open gas station will present itself among the welter of Christmas-closed shops crowding the street.

Then I notice the sign: St. Mary's hospital. Yes, a hospital. They are open on Christmas Day. They are open every day irrespective of—or perhaps because of—the holy birthday . . . As I enter the building my eye is caught by a headline in a nearby vending machine: *US and Iraq trade harsh war threats.*

I'm sitting in the car, cold on this clear Christmas Day. The sun was in my peripheral vision when I began writing this account yet now brick buildings block its light—from my face and eyes only. I see light along rock ledge, the rising lawn of brown winter grass and dirt. Trees jut out of rock crevices. A clutter of thin lit twigs, graceful turnings, still and full.

I'm looking at rock. The hilllock rises—rock, laced with pegmatite sills and dikes. It rises into rock heaps, implacable. These rise into a structure of rock, regular and cemented into a straight wall. This, in turn, rises into massive precision, a mighty building of cut stone. Its far end points skyward in two towers with eight spires of granite and slate. I'm looking at the object of my Christmas journey. The Church of Sts. Peter and Paul in downtown Lewiston. And I'm here solely because of its cold, mighty, majestic, formidable *looks*. On second thought, also because I want to record them. When I first saw them the effect was like that of the massive Berlin New Hampshire pluton upon me: I was nudged awake by that solitary, massive, great, frozen granite rock. Plutons push up, molten, moving all above them, upper layers fall, eroding away.

There is a cold breeze outside our car, though nothing moves but a plastic rag knotted on a tree limb, a twig. One slender naked beauty spindly above me across from the car. Just so light, the rag floats on an otherwise nonexistent breeze available to any eye passing or peeping out the nursing home window. I'm parked below the Church between it and a nursing home, waiting for Mass to begin. I don't recall ever being in a Catholic Church before.

All over New England, in most all the old once-successful mill towns, one finds these astonishing structures in brick or stone. One day this before me will be christened a basilica. Now it is a reminder that those coming across the border, the French-Canadian immigrants, gave unstintingly out of a bounty of labor not well-paid. For these workers, especially, often were not well-treated . . . and in Yankee communities they were despised.

Stirring on the radio is Handel's *Messiah*, rousing me to meaning, revealing this day a reminder of something that hasn't happened in my sight. It's another working day to me, to my spouse, to the other paper mill workers and those in the nursing home opposite, nursing.

Two gray-haired women approach a pale yellow car, one of them unlocking it. The rag has stopped blowing momentarily. A man with cane also comes up to the car, goes to the passenger door, front, and slides carefully in. The woman driver starts the car and they pull out. The torn end of rag on its tree drifts out a little. A rich mellow and sad feminine voice sings, "He was despised," and "He hid not his face from shame and spitting."

The structures opposite—Church of Sts. Peter and Paul—have my attention. Everything is formed from rock, rock that soars up out of a base of fixed chaos, grading into strong and strengthening regularity; thence into a yet more precise form of buttressing and towers and spires, sharp points piercing the sky. "He was despised . . . rejected."

Then, "Surely he has borne our grief and carried our sorrows . . ."

This structuring cries out to be photographed, drawn, painted. It cries out to be an image. And it is. It is the mightiest image going here. So much so it has drawn me out of the sleep of a household in rural mountains to descend into a city simply—so that I might look up at it on Christmas Day.

I'm not Catholic, I've never been to Mass. But I am here and will enter into the stone image of might and belief solely because, as I look up at the rocky lawn, strewn with the shadows of naked trees, it seems . . .

I enter the sanctuary and note sales of prayers for the Middle East on a table . . . feel helpless contempt . . . Should pray for the Middle East . . . I'm seated in the deep-vaulted half of this sanctuary on a maple-stained wooden bench, solitary among a scattered congregation. The Mass has not begun, I look around, take notes of what I see, hoping no one will be offended by it.

At the head of the sanctuary is a white-clothed altar, banks of white and red poinsettia spread before it in keeping with this season. Behind is a large Christmas tree, lighted in white, cardboard cutouts, structures of angels on either side with trumpets. Throughout this height and depth are pillars adorned with wreaths. Behind the large crucifix in a corner is a crèche or Nativity, surmounted by a lit star.

Low thunder of an organ sounds. I feel it vibrate in my lone body, seated in the midst of the sanctuary. I turn to look at mighty pipes in the rear, noticing scattered worshipers behind me. More worshipers are arriving, taking places either in front or behind me, but the middle section, where I sit is mostly empty. An old man, smooth and bald on top, wearing a hearing aid, sits down two pews in front of me on the aisle. Everyone wears a coat because it's cold in this cavern of cut stone . . . as, I suppose, it was in the old cathedrals of Europe, where there were no pews . . . where people came to stand or kneel in worship.

A man in a white robe (surplice?) standing near the altar begins speaking in French. Perhaps he's the priest . . . ? Liquid sounds of a language I don't know issue from him. A nun draped in black is now directly in front of me, but at a distance. She is front, among the congregation sitting close to the altar. I note, during the entire course of the Mass, that she remains kneeling throughout. Another priest, wearing a white robe adorned with crosses, stands and leads the congregation. Its singing is barely audible. His hand tries hard to lift the sluggish voices in melodious French song, rarely succeeding.

Peripherally I'm noticing movement and turn to see a procession moving up the aisle. It is led by a man in a business suit holding high a closed book. Behind him walks another with brass censor, lightly a'swing. Somehow the sight of a man in business suit bearing a book in worship or carrying a container of incense moves me. It takes time . . . before the exotic richly flowered odor reaches me. They're almost to the altar before I sense it. The incense reminds me of ancient biblical rites, prayers, and purified censors. Yet neither the book nor the incense means anything more to me, so ignorant of this ritual.

There comes a responsive reading in French. The parishioners, young, old and middle-aged take part. There are only one or two children present among them.

The man in suit reads from the book; he holds it up for us to see. There's a response from parishioners as they apparently comment upon the book in French. Then we rise and the people sing. The nun in black remains kneeling.

One of the white robed men who came up the aisle begins to speak at the pulpit. I recognize very few of the words. One, for instance, pronounced "grass." This is grâce. I remember it from a poem I once memorized in French:

"grâce pour toi-même
et grâce pour moi."

"Mercy for you/and mercy for me."

I recognize also the words "Mexico, Maine," "Noel" and "question." These are the fluid sounds of the language I enjoy listening to, without understandin . . . Still I hear.

He ends and leaves the sanctuary by a back door.

We rise and there follows a reading in unison, a more responsive reading. Now it's time for the collection. I reach for my purse, somewhat embarrassed. Sometimes I travel, out of necessity, with little cash, especially after buying presents for the holiday. I have only a little coin in my wallet along with a Christmas check to give J. D.: contribution for his snow tires. I'm relieved to hear occasional jingles as the laymen pass with collection bags on long handles. When one comes toward me I add my sound to the accumulation of bills, envelopes, change.

One of the priests washes his hands in a bowl held by one of the suits (laity). We stand and the congregation joins in song *a cappella*. Three priests stand behind the altar. Now one in the middle holds something and then others on either side hold out a hand, each toward the objects as though indicating or, perhaps, honoring them. I assume these faraway things are the emblems of the Lord's Last Supper; that this is the ritual in which they are transmuted into his body and blood that these might be taken in on the human tongue.

A kind of drowsiness slips upon me; a feeling of deadness, inattentiveness. A coffee letdown, I guess. Suddenly worshipers begin shaking hands with one another. The man two pews away looks at me tentatively, half-dismissively. I move toward him and take his hand. It is soft in mine, soft as my grandmother's was. The congregation moves, pouring into the aisle like so many colored beads, pouring toward the altar. I stay where I am. The priest has drunk from a golden cup. The old smooth man with whom I've shaken hands also remains seated as communicants partake of emblems of sacrifice. We, then, are unconfessed, joint communicants in our nonparticipation. The holy supper ends, and everyone is now back in his or her place.

The man with the book returns down the aisle, holding it high, celebratory. Now, as he passes in the procession, I see the great gold letters upon its front: *Lectionaire Du Dimanche*. Roughly: Lessons for Sunday.

Comes the benediction. The congregation disperses. I walk up the aisle toward a side door marked exit. There a gray-haired man extends his hand. His smiling bespectacled eye is gentle and glad—surprised—drawing the same spirit from me.

He *is* surprised. "Merry Christmas," he says, glad I am here, a stranger.

"Merry Christmas," I return, slightly disappointed that the exchange is in English. I chose the 11 a.m. Mass because it was in the language of French.

Real People in an MTV War

When I awoke it was 11° below zero. Sat in the dark of our bedroom drinking coffee and thinking of my former neighbor. *Nancy* was the American version of her name; she was a Palestinian refugee/immigrant in the late 1970s when we met. Sitting in this darkened room, beside my sleeping husband, warm cup of coffee in my hands, I recall every experience with Nancy that I can think of.

The war with Iraq is one week old. I sat hoping tensions between Arabs and Americans wouldn't escalate to a point where my friend and her family would suffer here in the USA—where she now lives and makes her home. Nancy had no home now in old "Palestine"—as it was known to her. She never said anything bitter about the fact that Israel displaced the Palestinians as once these had displaced Israel.

We never discussed this ancient quarrel, we never discussed the politics. We talked culture, we talked mothering, we talked very little of anything else. She told me about the Palestinian, I told her about the American, customs. And we talked of mothering because we were both young mothers.

I've always thought of her as courageous. When I first saw Nancy standing on her porch surrounded by massive hunks of ice which had taken down the electric—box, lines and all . . . It was a fierce Midwestern winter, bitterly cold, ice building up on everything. Ice outside her apartment house had fallen with violence, shaking our two buildings. We came rushing out of our respective houses to find the cause. That's when I first saw this brown young mother from a strange land—a *much* warmer land—surrounded by ice. We stood on our separate porches looking down at the ice. It had pulled down telephone wire as well. I was dumbfounded, and under the impression she could not understand English. I don't remember how I got this idea. Suddenly she asked, in unmistakable accents, if I had a phone she could use. She may have asked twice before I responded with a yes and an invitation. She came with two small brown children in tow.

After this we visited sometimes, but our friendship didn't heat up until the weather did. Then it blossomed forth in our semi-comfortless apartments.

On food culture we exchanged recipes. I told her how to make beef stew. She taught me how to make a dish of ground meat, rice, and onion rolled up in cabbage or grape leaves. We got pretty excited when the leaves came out in our backyard and discovered the neglected tangle of grape vines—joyous in being able to use this substitute for pricier tasteless cabbage. Nancy's Mediterranean fare included a rich almost whey-less yogurt made simply with whole milk and drained to produce a thick spread-able cheesiness. She gave me some sandwiched in Lebanese bread with olive oil. Marvelous. She gave me espresso, dark and rich. She gave me something I'd never seen: *ripe* figs, yellow and juicy.

Once Nancy asked her brother to take her out to dinner so she could sample American food. She had fried chicken. When I asked how she liked it, she shook her head. I wondered why fried chicken would be unappealing until I learn he had taken her to The Standard fast-food chicken. Then I felt sorry that this was her intro to traditional southern cookery.

The memory I most enjoyed, while sitting in bed with coffee, was what I think of as quasi mythological incident. It gave me as much a feeling for Nancy's culture as the food. Her children were a little girl, and a boy, two years old. Mohammed was a fetching curly-headed toddler with light hair and light eyes in comparison with his dark eyed, dark-haired shy sister, age four.

Nancy had taken off his pants so he could go potty. But then Mohammed refused to put the pants back on. Standing in the living room by the open front door, she coaxed him, but still he refused. Then Nancy gestured toward open sky beyond the screen and said something to him in Arabic. Immediately the child came and put on his pants.

I was so amazed. And a bit envious. How did she do that, I wondered. How did she draw such a keen reasonable obedience—immediate—from that unreasonable being, a two-year-old?

"What did you say to him?"

Nancy gave an embarrassed laugh. "I tell him, 'put on the pants' or I call a big black bird to come—bite off his . . ." She gestured.

Well I guess that *was* reasonable, for a two-year-old. And I would never have been able to use such a method on my own children, but it gave me a fine enjoyment in Nancy's execution of old world mothering. And I was in awe at the speed of Mohammed's compliance.

At 5:40 it was time to put away the memories, set down the coffee, and rise. I walked over to the digital thermometer: -13.5°F. then took a flashlight and went downstairs to fix breakfast. While Allen dressed, the temperature dropped to -14. While canned hash was heating, I slipped out into the cold where a nearby forest tree cracked and popped in these subzero temperatures; started our car and backed it out of the rickety garage. I wanted to warm it for the long drive to Rumford. Looking up through the windshield I saw Allen with his coat on at the front door of the house . . . about to heat up the car. I'd beat him to it.

The sun was still sunk in the Dantesque cold of night as we approach the paper-mill town, its surrounding hills just beginning to prove themselves— vast humped silhouettes against predawn pale cold air. My mind had returned to memories of my Palestinian friend.

Down by the river, running hidden alongside the highway, low alders stood rimed in ice. Not a thick heavy version seen in mountain photos, but the pale delicate delineation of frost vapor. Vapor rose in a still dance from alder thickets, hinting the Andy River's presence.

I looked up, across the opposite side of this highway. Rumford Hill rose in houses, tiers bristling with frost on naked trees, frost on many of those houses in the still dark. The street lights and other lights made this frosty snow-covered Hill resemble a lighted birthday cake, aglow in dim twilight.

We descended into town then crossed an arched suspension bridge. Frost vapor off adjacent falls and river poured through the breach, enveloping us and headlights of oncoming traffic; gleaming through a roiling fog. An illuminated mist moved hastily through this still mysterious light.

War was on the radio. War news, war highlights, war censored and manipulated, that newly minted phrase, "collateral damage." We pulled into a turn at the corner of route 108 and drove deeper—past massive log and chip piles toward employees' parking and the Lower Gate. Mountainous piles were covered with rime ice from the roiling vapor of great paper-making machinery. Vapor arose from the mill's massive structures in a vast body as though from a monolithic cauldron. Ridges of logs, rising on either side of a flume deepened the cleft of this river valley—all things coated in white and cold to the sight of a dwarf human, as we drove past.

After dropping Allen off, I crossed the mysterious vaporous arched bridge again. Pushing accelerator to the floor, I climbed the birthday cake hill to river level above waterfalls. A couple miles up the highway I turned in at a sign of the yellow arches, pulling up to the window for more hot coffee.

The attendant is quick to get my change, hand over my coffee, and close the drive-up window. The thick cloudy sky is vast, beginning to glow like cold red wine, but Fahrenheit degrees will still be negative for several hours to come.

I pulled over before heading onto the highway, lifted the drink-while-you-drive tab on my plastic cup, added cream. The radio was pouring out the war. Its news meshed with memories of my refugee friend. It was to be a Holy War, declared Saddam Hussein. Driving down the highway, reflecting upon its complexities of corporate-and-oil motives, passions, terrifying weaponry, and helpless casualties, I realized that he was right. It would be a holy war.

I pushed another button on the radio, looking for music or anything else. A snappy morning-talk duo deplored the poorly equipped Iraqi tanks: "They're not wired with MTV." I flipped back through to the news station. Here was a discussion of prisoner-of-war training school tactics for our soldiers and airmen. If captured: Survival, evasion, resistance, escape—SERE for short.

A half-hour later I pulled up to my cold weather destination: ski slopes of Sunday River, got out and went into the lodge for a few moments. When I came out I found my car blocked by other cars that had parked out of zone. I was surrounded by the cars of skiers here for a date of subzero pleasure on the steep slopes. My errand here was over but I couldn't move.

I sat in the car, listening to news radio, thinking of Nancy, looking up at these mountains where long white swaths trail down forest-dark flanks like wounds.

It's cold outside the car, making everything brittle. As if a stiff kick could shatter some tree without damaging the foot. I could crack one of those blocking cars, thin and hollow, with a karate chop. The substance of everything seems a façade. Were I to shove a hunk of snow with my foot, it would skitter across the snow-cast like a piece of Styrofoam.

Not as that ice which fell like granite shaking our two houses, starting a friendship.

It's a holy war. All wars are. But here it is made for TV.

Moony

I'm sitting at my desk/table in the dark, looking out our upstairs window at moonlight/shadows in the landlord's backyard. The moon itself is above and behind, shining, no doubt, upon the front of the house and into the street. I am in the dark about the moon—is it coming or going? rising or setting?—but think I may find something out simply by watching shadows cast by things blocking its light.

Though I have admired its great beauty, I haven't paid much attention to the moon over the course of my life. Its movements are mysterious and hard for me to comprehend. Yet, I perceive it to be mighty with metaphor in all aspects—its orbits, phases, its spatial and earthly interactions, and in its quality of light. It is worth quite a bit to me for mystification and metaphor alone. But more than this, I believe that the Moon is worthy simply for its own sake. It could exist without saying anything figurative, a prize beyond measure.

Below me, out the window, I see its great spread reflection gleaming up in white splendor of snow. Dark lacing shadows, thick and thin, lie upon shimmers of fair whiteness. Wispy shadow-lines streak the yard falling beneath bare deciduous branches gleaming above. The thrown contour of roof is peaked and dark. I know the lines of this structure itself are straight, but below me its shadow is clipped and gouged. This is because of the pocked condition of snow, old snow, perhaps a week old. Footprints have dented the surface and I descry them because of shadows on dents closest to the source of light.

Looking into the woods I see much gleaming through these naked trees. Where hemlocks stand, all is thick shadow, bottoms of trees merging with this shadow. Writing of what I don't know is like these things merging with shadows. Experience (with observation), making connections, researching: These three bring out the creative nonfiction. If even one is missing it's not finished.

My moon-shadow watching is interrupted when I'm called out of the house on an errand. Once in the street I look up through twiggy trees at the shining disc, itself pocked by mountains and craters, footprints of giants, upon its old surface. It is waxing toward the full, according to my calendar, in three nights. The orb is in its accustomed place high in the eastern sky.

When I return to our dark upstairs room and take my place by our window the sharp peaked and gouged roof shadow is gone. It has moved, diminishing as the moon rises, drawing closer to the house. I look around at other shadows and understand these are slowly creeping beneath objects casting them—beneath house, tall pine trees. Unlike the sun, which it reflects, the moon in winter appears to rise higher in the sky, casting short shadows, like those of noon in summer. This light, though cold and wan in comparison to a winter noon's sunlight is, nevertheless, light of the sun coming to us from a body that has no light of its own. The reflected light reaches our upturned eyes in varying shapes, depending on relative positions of earth, moon, and sun.

Phases of the moon reference this. In them we are treated to the spectacle of a body of (reflected) light waxing, waning, and disappearing altogether in the shapeless dark. Even though our lunar lamp orbits our earth in 27 days, its cycle of phasing takes 29 days, 12 hours and 44 minutes according to my sources. In this cycle primitive cultures saw the metaphor of aging, death and rebirth. By it they understood that life continues and death is an appearance (or disappearance), albeit a mighty one. And dark. The new moon is a dark one, reflecting no light to our eyes.

The failure and fullness of this light is gradual, increasing from no light through crescent, quarter and gibbous phases to full, strong and healthy. These descriptors, according to Jamie Jobb's *Night Sky Book*, are those of South African bushmen. Again, the moon possesses no light in itself, yet it reflects because of its position, its relationship—a full measure of light in the midst of the phasing cycle.

At least that's how it appears to our eyes. If we could move off planet and around we would see then that it is always a fully reflecting surface, except when eclipsed by some other body.

The quarter phase appears to my eyes as half a moon. It is one quarter of the way through the trip around our earth. The crescent phase is frequently shown a circle of light fully rimmed in thick and thin light. Thick where lies the crescent, thin where earthshine reflects from it back at us. In this case it is a treble redounding of sunlight.

For all its phases, the moon has a greater array of appearance beyond that of waxing and waning glory. Earlier in the midst of night I saw it low-lying, westward in quarter phase, on its side. Like a half open eye gleaming through clouds. The following afternoon it was in the east, high and wan because the sky was light blue, wasting it.

One night has passed, and a day. The moon is risen. I go to my son's empty room to look upon the moon-made landscape. I'm tired, weary from to-day's labor. All I want is rest. The moon is there, the land gleams white: snowy house across the street, snowy yard, snowy road. Cold and frosty light. I move slowly back along the hall toward an upstairs room where I work, and where I sleep with Allen.

Now Allen is at the desk studying instrument flight rules. I think this poor man would like to have a Mooney. Lamp-glow upon the page, and his entrenched presence at the desk, give me pause. I will not be able to sit there in the dark tracking shadows. I sit on the bed contemplating the situation:

I'm not done with the moon. I know the moon is not done with me. Tomorrow night and the next night and maybe for nights thereafter the forecast is for clouds. My head is heavy, drooping toward the bed. I follow it to lie upon my side. It feels so good. It feels like I should come to bed now, sleep. And I could be excused, the day has been long. Should I fight it?

Well, what if this were my last chance? My chance for moonlight if forecasts come true. Or what, even, if I were never to see the moon again? Ever.

Now I'm out on the snowy road, gritty salted, sanded in the moonlight. And I am still thinking that thought. Ancient prophecies could come due in my lifetime. The moon may one day be blotted out for my eyes. And, barring that, I will die and these eyeballs will see it no longer. But if my moony primordial inklings come true I will see it again thereafter . . . with other eyes, new eyes. (Not figurative; literal new eyes.)

Walking uphill, I tilt my head back, way back. The moon, not quite full, is high. I see it through clusters of twigs, appearing as a great shining white spider seated in the midst of its web. The encircling webbing is caused by moonlight reflecting off twigs in circular fashion.

I walk to a gap in the trees and tilt my face to see its lunar face without interference. Facial characteristics are clearly seen: its shadows of mountains and craters. Its face tilted downward toward mine.

I turn my back and look down. There is my foreshortened shadow on this snowy shoulder of our mountain road. It's a stubby or squat looking shadow, imperceptibly creeping under my form as the moon continues rising.

Feet planted, I turn my form from side to side, this way and that. My shadow-shoulders tilt up and down: slanted left and right/left and right, as I turn.

I walk on, looking for moon's shadows. Come to a snow machine track leading off the shoulder into logging paths, a large snow-covered clearing full of lunar light. Follow this track. It's a slung trail of tight ripples, flanked by smooth parallel tracks on either side. I can see these ripples because of their moon-shadows. Follow this track as it loops back toward the road.

Reluctant yet to head home, full of new life and no longer weary, I continue up the long hill, moon-musing as I climb. The moon seems an unreliable thing, erratic in movement, wasting and waxing. Yet we know that its movements are as precise as the sun's. As far as I know all heavenly movements are so, according to physical laws operable on them. I pass flanking woods, noticing, not for the first time, that the stationary trees appear to move—at differing rates of speed. As I move, trees next the road are fast movers, trees gleaming out of further woods appear to move slowly. I tilt back, watch the moon as I pass trees. It appears to move not at all. Rather the trees pass before it. Yet I do not leave it behind. We are keeping the same pace, companions; and these trees are moving in various speeds. The greater the distance of these things, the slower they seem to move in relation to me. It is as though I am standing still and things close are quickly moving, things further move slower, and the moon, furthest yet, moves not at all.

Perception is strange: that time and relative position should make such difference in the appearance of things . . . The moon turns out to be a steady-body after all . . . now that I've taken my last chance to see it.

Guaranteed-Learn-to-Ski

The resort owner has local public-relations in his pockets. He's a friend to the community, keeping resentment at a local minimum by providing jobs and inviting the community to partake of this resort enjoyment. All a person need do is be brave, show up on the doorstep of the resort on a local free-ski-day, and present herself.

Bravery is essential or, in the case of children, lack of fear will suffice. The less vanity in this situation, the better. For one cannot fall without feeling foolish. When I first came to Maine I took a brief look at the sport. Would I be willing to shoot down a mountain at 60 miles an hour without a car around my body? The answer was no. Only the brave, only those who found something appealing in having long pieces of composite materials clamped to their feet could answer yes to such a question.

So when, while working on a book about winter, the opportunity to take up the burdensome question presented itself in the form of a free ski day, I did not bother to lunge at the chance. Instead, I sat in bed mulling the question and drinking coffee to bolster my flaccid courage. Just about the time I had decided that I could ignore the question, I got a phone call from the neighbor-girl.

She was asking if I wanted to take her and three or four—or was a five?—kids to the free ski. "No," I said. "I've got work to do." Like a polite child, she thanked me and hung up. I spent another five minutes mulling the question: should I call her back and submit? Finally I decided to stick to my work, though it meant denying them the opportunity.

Another local day. You have to know it's only for the writing—*Maine Metaphor*. Had put it off as long as I could, then rose early to take Allen to work. I would have our car to go try this thing—although I wouldn't be able to wear it while skiing. And now I must initiate motions that would ultimately lead to that end. (That's one of the problems with going through motions.)

First the ski pants—insulated fat gray things borrowed from my son, J. D.. Let's see, I have a hat and mittens, and—whoops—I have no ski parka. Oh well, back to the desk . . . or to bed: I'll just to stay home after all. Then, hanging on a peg by the front door—J.D.'s old insulated jacket; with numerous pockets in which to stash things like ID (for the free ski), lip balm, car keys, money for lunch, and notebook. After putting it on I noticed its grubbiness. Then I remembered it had been used by the men in our house to change the oil of their various cars. There was a particularly telling fresh oil stain curving around the right lower sleeve. J.D., who came down with his ski gear ready to take off in his own car, said it would be all right: I'd be a local person, that's all. An insignificant speck of gray amid an imported state-of-the-art sea of blinding neo-fluorescence.

Another half-hour's procrastination and, twelve miles later, I stood in the community lift-ticket line. Standing in front of me were a ragtag bunch, the neighbor girl, her parents and four or five friends.

On learning I'd never worn a pair of skis, the ticket taker directed me to the Guaranteed-Learn-to-Ski office in the lodge. Once in, and following a video introduction for would-be skiers, I had a fitting for ski boots and skis with the instructor—named Phillips.

The skis, I couldn't help noticing, were short compared with skis one saw lined up on racks, or attached to the confident feet of the other-worlders. Phillips said it was easier to learn on short skis. I asked what the difference was and he said long skis glided better and gave more control on the slopes. "Then why are short skis easier to learn on?" As an impertinent beginner, I needed ease and control. But longer skis have sharper edges, are more likely to get caught . . . on something? New skiers don't have enough strength to control their legs with long floppy skis. So "shorter skis are easier for beginners."

Then I found myself walking around the sun deck with my feet and lower legs encased in ski boots. The ski boots made me feel part robot. Walking was not something I took for granted now, especially, walking on ice; which is what my group had to do before climbing onto the Guaranteed-Learn-to-Ski truck.

Standing in the back of the truck, waiting for our instructor, I noticed a large white ambulance pulled up to the front. A crisp white stretcher hustled into the lodge. I leaned toward another student and said, "You don't see equipment like that parked outside the bowling alley."

The truck trundled off with us to an instruction area over the crowded road, cars parked everywhere. Condos packed in neat blocks inside a fringe of woods. We learners exchanged info on home locations: a couple from Booth Bay Harbor Maine, two women friends over from Mass., a couple from Vermont, one from Connecticut; a blonde from out-of-state somewhere. She had the same name as my own and a pair of ill-fitting ski boots. The two Mass women had some cross-country experience. Turns out I was the only free-going local in the group.

The instruction area, slightly undulant in mini slopes, was cordoned off with pink fluorescence strips on poles, located just off the bunny slopes afloat with happy-limbed colors. A reckless bunny could plow into us, I noted, looking up at the slope curving away above us.

Before donning skis Phillips told us to practice sidestepping up-slope and down in the boots. This was to be the method of ascending while wearing skis. Turn by making a right angle of your feet. He lined us up and we laid out our skis. He then showed us a plate on the bottom of our ski boots and demonstrated how to slide it between bindings and *stamp* it—locked—into place. We locked on one ski. It wasn't as easy as it looked. Nothing was to be that easy. The first time everything *looks* easier than it is—the way first times are. After some instruction and practice things can be easy as pie, but even pie is difficult if you don't know how to make it.

I lifted a ski at the end of my foot and tried waggling it side to side as Phillips was instructing. It felt like a heavy, artificial and extensive protuberance that should be disengaged, lopped off as soon as possible. We were expected to move with something like that on our bodies? Phillips next enjoined: "Try turning with the ski on; good. Now turn the other way." To my surprise—I could actually move.

Step #1: learn that you can move. I looked off happily at the colorful bunnies, many little ones among them, who glided past us on short slopes beside the instruction area. I was making great strides: now for the other ski.

We practiced the sidestep up and down a slight incline, learning that an edge could be rolled inward, digging, for the brake. Phillips now taught us how to make "the wedge." By turning the tips toward one another, pigeon-toed, our skis would slow. By spreading legs, widening the angle between skis, we could slow more. Finally, when the wedge was wide enough, and applied with force, we could stop on the slight slope. Initially, learning to stop, then, must be the most important lesson. "Look, Mom; I can stop."

Knowing how to make the wedge, and its importance, were not the same as actually executing the wedge while sliding down-slope. My legs were going to have to learn this through repetition and strengthening. What to do with my poles while en route was another ticklish matter. Gliding down-slope, suddenly I'd be aware of their presence in my hand, dragging; dragging behind or hanging down.

Phillips was telling us the importance of balance. He said the tendency of beginners is to pull back, as though to say, "I don't want to go down there." This reminds me of flying: The yoke must be pushed forward to save oneself in a stall, but the tendency is to pull back. But in order to maintain balance we must lean forward, shins into our boots.

One by one we tried wedges with angles of varying degrees; we tried wedges turning left, wedges turning right. We were getting the feel of these wedges. Maybe. My sense of security on skis vacillated almost moment by moment. One moment okay, the next unsure.

Skis make falling a lot harder than falling was meant to be. Falls are wrenching because of the rigidity of skis and boots. After accidentally "learning" to fall I learned I didn't know how to get up again. Foolish falling is nothing to the ego compared with the inability to rise again. To struggle like a fish out of water with legs encased in concrete and feet lengthened to monstrous proportions. To lack strength enough to push on the locking mechanism and thus release these offending appendages. One struggles thusly while fellow students, almost equally clumsy, are gliding toward one. Someone helped me up—another instructor—and afterward Phillips instructed us in how to rise after a fall. The easiest way is (characteristically enough) the silliest looking. The prone spread eagle affair in which the butt rises while ones hands walk backwards. Fun.

Phillips has decided we've had enough of that. He leads us, wedging this way and that, down to the next instruction area with obstacles for turning points.

And again I fall, but this time, desperately trying to avoid the spread eagle butt-rise method, I muster strength enough to push on the locking mechanism and release it. My ski comes away, I stand and, being careful to align my form sideways on the slope, prop myself with the pole and neatly snap the ski back onto the boots. Quickly I start the exhausting sidestep back up slope. I'm beginning to tire. The skis seem somehow heavier than before, my legs shakier.

Top of the slope, and I begin to pray. My confidence in wedges, in my 43-year-old ability to do anything resembling skiing is suddenly gone. If I push off now I'm liable to land in the adjacent gully among trees or in its stream. (Suddenly close.) Looking over at it, I try not to imagine how many would-be skiers have landed down there.

Suddenly a friendly voice says, "Your stance is too knocked-kneed." I looked away from the gully to see another instructor standing before me. "You need to execute your wedge with a wider spread of the knees, of the thighs. Use the thigh muscles for stability. That's it. Feel the stability? Now try it."

Slowly I descend, the new instructor going before. "Look up, look at my face. Don't look at your feet. To descend, look where you're going, not at your feet."

Something like looking and listening to God when trying to sequence nonfiction chapters.

I followed his face down-slope, navigating orange cones, and found my way to the bottom with ease. I was amazed. Those few words correcting my posture and drift, the sight of that face—all the difference.

"Your feet will follow the line of your sight. You want to see where you're going in order to get there."

If I look down, I'm more likely to go down because that's where I'm looking. I'm looking at the instructor's name tag. "John." A name that means "God is gracious."

Again the sidestep up hill. I'm anxious to try more but there's so much to remember. I overhear Phillips telling a student to turn across the slope in order to keep his speed down before attempting the next turn. Then, as I get ready to ascend again, John comes up and says, "Grip your poles like you would a lunch tray, out in front, elbows bent."

Slowly he led me down-slope again with simple instructions: "Press with your right big toe when you want to go left. That's it. Feel that toe work? Now with the left toe to turn right. That's it!"

The body is suddenly in orchestration with each member playing its little part as though on cue. Slowly at first—then, at some future time, say, after more practice, with more confidence and gained agility—skiing would be a practiced symphony, interwoven of all the instrumental components.

These may be silly unpracticed arms and legs, but with practice, persever-ance, and instruction, this body may yet perform.

But not today: John says it's after one o'clock: time for this would-be skier to turn back into a local and go pick up her husband at the mill.

Inside the rental room I spy one of my fellow students, the blonde with the same name as mine. She has returned for better fitting boots and I recall she had complained of pain from the ill-fitting ones. My eyes widen in surprise at the severity of an injury from skiing in wrong-size boots. The boots left her feet bleeding!

"I guess you need to really cry out loud before the instructor under-stands that you're hurt," I say sympathetically. I once injured my ankle ligaments in aerobics class: tore and jarred the elasticity right out of them because on top of the initial injury I kept after the exercise. Just kept doing it when I should have quit. Stubbornness in pursuit of perfection is my misguided way of life.

On the way out I see Crystal with her family: the postal worker in our village. We smile and agree that free ski days are good for the community. Going ahead I note more community people. Some are turned out in bright colors like those from out-of-state; some are dressed in the drab colors of a few seasons back. And some are here in holey jeans and thin coats.

Wearily I go look for the car. Yeah. The car.

Squirrelly

Marginalia: check December paper (front) for weather info. Also check the log for lows.

It is winter. Five or six weeks remain between me and a calendar spring. According to local lore four or five months will lapse until we bask in Maine's only other season—July.

Allen said our mild winter would force corresponding aberrations in another part of the world, the Middle East. Turns out the weather in Europe and England and in the Mediterranean *has* been uncharacteristically harsh. I determined yesterday to sit here today and observe, remember, and write. It was to be a snow-stormy day, an unusual weather day for the '90–91 season. Both December and January were mild months. February has been mild so far, with few exceptions of below zero nights. The jet stream *is* streaming straight across-country from the west instead of originating out of the north, dipping southward, shooting north again as it does this time of year. Outside the upstairs window an occasional whirlwind clouds the air with blustery snow, very fine grained.

Nothing is stirring in the white yard below. Fat squirrels are elsewhere at the moment. Allen wondered if mild weather accounted for their sleek glossiness. The red species appear no fatter than usual. I chased the grosser grays off our bird feeder by the kitchen window with a broom. Washing a plate, I looked up to see another swaying the cedar feeder while presumably stuffing its face. then only its thick fluffy white under-tail and fat rump were visible on the ledge of the feeder.

I like sitting up here in the bedroom at an antique worktable with angel-wing struts, watching little black chickadees thread their dipping way through woods, making for a feeder not visible from here. Their flight is undulant and indirect. It curls from tree to tree around perimeters of the open yard—as each makes its way toward food. Each chickadee is marked with a difference. They know each other and have a feeding hierarchy. I've seen it happen so: No bird will feed at the trough until the previous feeder flies off.

Later I looked out and saw a gray squirrel beneath the feeder, sorting through ground litter for discarded seed. Its fatness intrigued me. The fat was packed tightly beneath its taut skin from jaw line to rump. Its coat, glossy and full.

There is a spruce in these woods, or maybe a fir, larger than others nearby. I sit on our bed some mornings and see it tall in the distance, straight dark front visible through lower branches of the woods. Colors out there are nonexistent. There's only brownness, sometimes touched with white, filling the scene. Higher up a colorless silhouette of spruce is evident against sky—dull or bright. It's there I see the equally colorless silhouettes of fat squirrels jumping along its prickly length. Every morning they play about that tree.

I took a walk up Deer Hill after writing the above, discovering that the fine snow described was really sleet, delicate light fine pieces of ice drizzling dimly in failing light. On my left, as I crunched through white cover on our road, I saw dense tweedy woods—conifer in sleet and snow. Thick and dark. On my right the bristling new forest of deciduous saplings.

Sleet is caused by warm air heaving itself over high cold above the earth. Moisture falls through the cold, accreting into ice pellets. I heard about this warm air today. There was a thunderstorm south of here. In winter, not July?

Guaranteed-Taste-Humility

March 15, 1991

Marginalia: orchestration at the end of piece. Lots of good stuff in bio book on muscles and tendons—use it.

At last I am back at my table again, safe. Here I have practice and some skill. Here, to quote an academic authority, there's a bit of muscle. At this table, with this pen in my hand, I have some control. Some.

This morning, out of my milieu, I had seeming none of this. This morning I had no skill, no orchestration, no ability. And I was up on the flank of a mountain, discovering what one does have when these are absent in such a place. One has humility. Or, at least, humiliation.

It started fine, like any morning. A little sun, a little cloud, a warming trend underway. I began with the usual amount of confidence. Or maybe its edge was off just a bit. After all, I was going to try alpine skiing again. I had skied before, as these pages record. I had tried learning to ski. And I thought I was undeceived: I knew that my body was unpracticed, that the pattern of orchestration necessary to coordinate my members had not yet been established. I encouraged myself: it would come, with practice.

I took the highway, followed signs and the habit to the ski-way, parked our car and sat a moment looking up at North facing slopes. Over the years here in Maine those fair white ropes of sinuous trails, cut in fir-dark ridges, have been a godsend to my sons. (Even my spouse has had work upon this mountain, building condominiums with a contractor.) The white ways have provided our sons employment and recreation; provided them skill, pleasure, confidence, earned of their efforts and desire. Slopes taught their bodies more coordination and control than they would now otherwise possess.

I fiddled a moment with my clothing. Put on the wool shirt, decided to leave the coat on the backseat. A slight overcast sifted sun's rays but it would be another warm one, 40's anyway. I got out, slammed the door and slogged through mud past rows of vehicles. When I got to the end of the lot I took off my mittens and turned back. Really—too warm for mittens.

Up on the beginners' undulant slope with eight other students and Charlie, our instructor. Nearby skiers, many children, swished past on their way down-trail toward the lift. Some skiers gliding by were outfitted with strange gear. Some had skis on the ends of their poles instead of baskets. Some had skis lashed and locked into the wedge position. Others skied on sleds with guides. A nearby building was headquarters for the resort's adaptive ski program. Disabled persons learned to ski free. Watching them was an encouragement to me. If they could do it, couldn't I?

The skis felt heavier than I had remembered from my first lesson. Charlie demonstrated the wedge, configuration in which upturned tips of skis are pointed toward each other with tail ends wide apart, forming a V-shape. An unnatural position for those unused to it, requiring strength in the thighs and calves. To a student nearby: "I think the appropriate muscles have atrophied over the years," I might have said over the decades.

Marginalia: careful here, get it right. Insert paragraph or two on muscles.

I could recall, from my athletic childhood, no game or sport for which these particular muscles, and in this configuration, came into play. Or had I ever used them so before?

"To turn right," Charlie said, "press on the ball of your left foot. Feel the force of it in your left thigh. Keep . . . the . . . wedge. That is your brake. Use it."

And so we practiced. Here, I thought, is where I come into the skill. Practice will give me this wedge, this turn, this sport. *I would ski.*

One of the students kept applying the seat of her pants to the granular surface in order to stop herself. "Use that wedge," Charlie commanded. "That is your brake. Would you rip the brakes out of your car!?"

(And this has been my point in the past: down-mountain at sixty miles an hour without a car?)

After a couple of hours, I was growing weary of this wedging practice. It was time for my nap.

But Charlie seemed satisfied with our progress. It was time to take it to the lift, another new experience.

Apprehensive, we lined up, a colorful queue in the midst of less tentative colors—arriving skiers who actually possessed some skill. Skill enough to be whisked proficiently uphill beyond sight among treetops. Skill enough to arrive downhill, body and soul. Go fly!—back up and down again.

I was last in the line of students, had a lift to myself. It hit the back of my legs and I sank into it, held tight the poles, it lifted me away. Yanked down the bar and felt a little more secure as we rose on high. My skis felt heavier, dragging, weighting those boots at the ends of my legs. Hanging there. They turned outward and tended to cross behind. At first I forced my thews to turn them inward in parallel, but soon *decided* to relax. To rest and enjoy the unusual experience of physical flight. I was very tired.

Marginalia: signs on the way up mountain: "skiing to endanger"—"skier to be removed".

Warning signs posted on poles above eye level squelch my enjoyment as I pass. We are warned about the dangers of skiing and urged to ski safely. Stories of devastating injuries pass through my mind: the schoolboy who had languished in a coma, the man who crashed, spread eagle, into a tree at seventy miles an hour. I recalled the first-aid stations, ambulance lanes and stretchers of an earlier trip to the resort. These thoughts were wise ones and did not daunt me. My weak legs might, however. Could I have practiced the wedge *too much*?

And then the lift was slowing, shooting me off like an ace onto the granular surface. The group was to my left on a knoll above a slight decline which joined larger trails, spreading out of sight in all directions. Charlie, wise instructor, told us to have a race: See who could go slowest.

And then we were off, one by one. The slope was different from those on which we practiced—very little flat. Sliding down I could see nowhere to stop, to rest my legs during the effort to hold the configuration: the wedge. My physical concert was fast deteriorating into cacophony, melodic line falling apart. I fell.

Tried to rise. One of the male students came back. Other skiers stopped to assist me getting to my skis. But the strength in my thews was gone. I couldn't even push myself onto my pathetic legs. Strength was in my arms, however. I pushed on the poles. Somehow, two men assisting, we got me to my feet.

But there was no holding me. The slope was, after all, a slope. And my carefully practiced wedge was gone. The shape of it still existed somewhat, but as Charlie discovered when he came to my aid, its force of application was gone.

Trying to save face, foolishly determining to go on, I apologized. "I must've left my confidence on the lift." It had stayed on the lift and gone down to the bottom without me. I almost used the word "nerve" for confidence—but the ego would not have it. Neither would the ego have me confessing my entire loss of the wedge.

Yet technically *nerve* was the right word. What I—human—undertake in accord with info processed by my senses depends upon my skeletal muscle, the "effectors" of motor and sensory neurons—my voluntary nervous system. The muscles were shot for the day, both confidence and nerve gone.

Marginalia: science or refer back. skiers coming down around me.

Charlie encouraged me to follow in the wake of his wedge but it was more than I could do. He went backwards, bent forward, going down-slope, toward his students waiting on another knoll, holding the tips of my skis trying mightily to brake this strange strengthless animal.

We stopped among the group, and I stood, mentally adrift. He gave them further instruction. I looked calmly out over the mountains, half listening, half considering my predicament. Then understanding came: I could not go down the mountain on skis. I took my pole, punched down on the release behind my boot and stepped out of the right ski.

Charlie looked over at me.

"Are you OK?"

"Fine," I said, suddenly aware that *I* was making *him* nervous. He continued to demonstrate while I stepped determinedly out of the left ski.

"Don't you have gloves or mittens?" someone asked a bit uneasily at my elbow. (Should you really be taking your skis off here on the mountainside?)

"Yes, in the car." (Would you mind going to get the car for me?)

Charlie finished and, as the group looked on, I told him I had no intention of going down on the skis. It was a psychically liberating moment. "And it's not the lack of confidence. These muscles are physically incapable of bringing me safely down the hill."

Ten minutes later, at mountain's bottom, I climbed out of a sled chained to a rackety snowmobile. It was one of the machines used to transport handicapped skiers. "Thanks," I said to the kindly old Mainer who helped me out in the middle of a curious crowd.

"I couldn't have got down without you." I said it loud enough for my ego to hear. Then I walked off on wobbling legs, lugging heavy skis and unwieldy poles toward the lodge.

I have decided to cut short my skiing career. I don't have time for the regimen required to build up my thighs, ankles and tendons; muscles. But the concert continues, for awhile, here at my table/desk. There I have a little muscle strengthened over the years by exercise.

Later, when I was beginning to wonder if my muscles had really been so weak on the slopes, I overheard J.D. talking to his dad on the phone. J.D. was home from school to take advantage of the free ski day. He hasn't been on the slopes but a couple times this winter. He said he quit early today.

"My legs feel like jelly," he said. (College freshman.)

Winter Gains and Loss

Monday 3–25–91

Four days into calendar spring. I will sit at my table looking out on thick wet white snow. I will trudge up Deer Hill in heavy boots. Kick at a threading pattern of white truck-tracks. I'll stare, silent, into black-and-white woven woods. They will be dense with the pattern, rod upon rod into woods below a dim white sky. Then later, in hazy sunlight, dark branches will begin dropping their white loads, pock the snow till it looks like a moonscape.

Spring is a time of inventory. We catalog the reawakening season. Lists of birds and insects and plants go on, go on as things emerge from sky overhead and mud below.

Marginalia: here begins winter of 91–92; November 12, 1991

I have felt winter coming, cleansing my nostrils while on the seashore. I have seen first flakes alighting in the city. Apprehensive and straining, I have ridden home through the storm; arriving safely at night in darkness so. . . .

Now, again, is winter and, if spring is a continuing record of gains out of doors, this is a season to number our losses. The walk taken last night, on our first real weather day of the bleak season, provided just such a record of debits.

The November day began in drenching rain, cold and sheeting. I listened, upon waking, to the sound of it on our roof overhead just above our slanted ceiling. Allen stood at the sole window in the room, watching. Wind swayed tall supple trees of leafless wood. Their thin naked twigs moved this way and that against the dim sky.

Marginalia: mention trying to decide if sleet or rain—looked at nearby ladder to determine; Kyle's ladder leaning against the house; not freezing on contact as would freezing rain.

Late in the day rain turned to sleet—pelting precipitation. Sleet fell and piled in low places in a sodden yard full of brown leaves and pine needles. It rolled into dents and dips collecting until full. Then these pellets began to smooth out all contours of this brown yard, whitening. I sat at my desk watching it hit, listening to the voices of my son and his friend Deborah, filtering up from the kitchen. I worry what her drive home will be like.

At night I went out in dark and thin falling snow. Sleet had softened and lightened, dribbling down as minuscule flakes. I unleashed the dog and, noticing a texture and feel of the storm-stuff underfoot, stepped into Deer Hill Road. Dim white lane had the consistency of brown sugar beneath my tread. It squashed and spread with every footfall.

Here was one gain I could name: the multiplicity of snow types. The Inuit, it's said, have perhaps two dozen words for as many types of snow, based (I would guess) on texture, size, moisture content, temperature and the like. We might lose myriad species of flowers to the cruel season but we gain a couple dozen kinds of precipitation.

As houses with neighbors fell behind, and light drained away, I began to count my losses. First, light was fairly lost. The dog had become a black shape moving over this dim gray lane before me. There was no color anywhere for the eye to seize, almost no value of shading. Trees had changed, our road was not the same. Shapes of trees, like flanking walls, match the dog in his dark colorlessness. A similar shadow being parallel lines of tire trails, led up the road. How is it possible that just a day before we had blue sky and the sheen of birch limbs, beige curls of beech leaves, the freshness of height, the height of an open sky? Not so long ago this road was full of leaf colors . . . before that of wildflowers and shimmers of green leaves. Now the lay of every line was different.

As with the road, this world was not the same. It impressed me with strange ambiguity. At once it seemed to close in and to recede around us. The old dog sensed it too, for he kept near, instead of bounding ahead as usual. We plodded through this strange snow, atmosphere close about us, raining snow on us, but managing nevertheless to keep remote. The sound of winds reached into my ears . . . but not down into my soul. Creation was keeping its emotional distance. I felt a muffling, nullifying, between me and the external, as of sensory deprivation. I set this down to a lack of light, and counted five senses as among the nominally lost.

In fact, they were receding along with the rest of creation, sympathetically, for lessening sight. I imagined I knew what it was to diminish slowly, sightless. It would take time for other senses to cease sympathizing and perk up. After darkness had been upon one, a while, they would kick out and begin carrying *more* of the sensory load than before.

I desired that this dark gray world would open itself to my senses and let me experience it, forcing myself to attend; deliver me from the tendency to trudge this road unaware. How could one tolerate the same old thoughts of such a different road and so different a world? How much less tolerable if all nights of this season were so? If, upon the first night, when winter's experience is still fresh, I found myself forgetful of it. How tedious nights to come after?

But now. The nights would not be like this. The nights would not line up like nutcrackers all wearing the same dreary pelting uniform. I would lose this special night, it would recede, never return, as surely as does each new experience.

Oh, if only I could reach out and grab you, seize you, stay you in my mind a while. You are dreary, a desolate and plodding night in the blowing wild. And I want every bit of you.

We climbed on and on to near the top where a view would have spread itself had it not been stolen. Sounds increased and the blindness must've lost its sympathetic companion, the auditory dullness. For, suddenly, rushing sounds filled my ears. Ah, here was a gain, even as I gained the heights: water running, pouring somewhere on either side of the soft squashy lane. The water had not yet been locked up in ice. *Hah*, it's only November; there's water running. Solid ice is still but a memory—of last winter.

Up on the flat, wind channels along the course of the road. I glance down and see to my surprise that I am coated in dim crystals, showing some valuation in place of my colorless coat. The dog, too, is coated with it, close by my legs.

"Come on Boots," I hollered. "Let's go down," and we turned and started down toward the house.

That's when I discovered another lost item: my footing in the gray sugar. "Lost" in these thoughts is relative. I do make my footing, it's not truly lost. But now I work to keep it, for my feet want to go out from under me. Gravity would hurry them along, but the strange precipitation is unearthing my balance. The elements *will*, whether I would or not. So I walk down the hill, negotiating every step; negotiating with a will of my own.

The road plunged down in ways and curves I'd not discerned before, or to which I had given little heed. One no longer desired to attend mysteries of the atmosphere, the falling of a cold wet sky, and the strange shadowy palings of the woods. I wanted only to get down safe, me and my dog. I wanted not to slide off some side ravine or break my behind in the fall.

These sweet curves and gentle slopes of yesteryear, when the road was the same road but so different, so safe. 'Twas but a season ago, or was it one week, perhaps? *No, 'twas yesterday when the sky was blue.*

We came down, the dog and I, back to houses and the sole street lamp, glowing pink. Now I counted my gains, so glad: the lights, real yellow lights of welcoming houses on a stormy night.

These houses, I thought. *Here is home, my great gain. For winter, you've come into your own; your confinement of four strong walls. You gain and grow, enlarging house, yellow light of ours.*

Diligently I've observed the year unwind, the season unraveling, divesting itself of autumnal gaiety and dash. Bright colored leaves so recently hollering for joy lie blackened underfoot. Today I saw them spread in black water in motley pattern of muted shadings. In late autumn our well water turns brown and dingy, stains the toilet bowl with tannin from fallen needles and leaves. We drive to the spring and load up with crystalline water. It flows beside the road forever while we sleep.

I walked the packed road, trunks of trees bristling thickly, woods full of squeaking, creaking, whistling and whirring: the rush of the grouse at my approach.

On the hill a road turned off my right shoulder, its own shoulders soft and frosted with snow. I followed till I came to a gravelly drive, caked with thin whiteness. We followed, the dog and I.

There I became aware of tracks of the deer, dainty. The heart-shape in white, edged in soft melt. Carefully I placed my feet over them and ground out each print. Erased each shapely heart.

The black dog followed and wove a dog track back and forth over our tracks, the deer's and mine. At times he stopped to sniff them. The dog is clean and brushed, clipped. He has had a bath and been de-tagged. All his matted clumps are gone. Brambles no longer trail from his behind. But he is going blind.

We tromped down toward the rounded slope of a ridge, coming out from many trees. So the view opened wide on mountains of the next town, spreading in patches of muted dark green, indigo, gray and brown; sifted with faint touches of white. Massive mountains seemed immortal, set forever beneath a restless moving sky. I stood staring while wind roamed on high, whistling. Then I looked down, turned around, searching for more tracks to squash.

There were no big tracks of the hunter here. I saw none until I returned to the road and followed it toward the ledge. We passed a great roadside puddle, milky with forming ice. Then, on the new extension leading to ledge, I saw large tracks, deeper, perhaps owing to the weight of a gun? But here were tracks of deer, overlain with these crude crushings. I made a mishmash of them for they remained visible, just delineated, inlaid with my own.

If a hunter (perhaps) comes after me and sees my mess and follows still, in spite of all, he's welcome to the deer. After all, the deer is wild and no possession of mine. Not my deer, no matter how I care.

Interlude

So ends the winter entries of *Maine Metaphor*, 1990–92. What follows is winter bearing toward the new millennium. We head into maturity, whether of soul or of insight you may judge. Old age cannot be called physical maturity. Has it psychic maturity, maturation of the soul? This maturation, if it is so, precipitates out of the past 15–25 years, from the mid-2000s into 2014.

After the following autumnal interlude, I will cull and place various entries from my everyday snow journals and my *reader's journals*, perhaps. All meld into themes of our winters in Maine. Winters since we stopped here, just so, at the beginning of our first winter—when the Salvation Army came to our rescue, and the in-laws, and our ancient friend, God. And then it might be good to cycle back to the beginning, to a flight in celebration of the New Year, new Maine life in the late 1980s. But also to reflect at last on the Big Winter: What is sometimes call Old Age.

We no longer live on the Deer Hill Road of the previous chapters, but, oddly enough, we live on the Deer Hill Road still—just over the ridge, Swans Ridge and Swan's Ledge. Into the next valley, it too named after the hill of those same old settlers who came here and built stony walls and raised a bit of stock and farmed this difficult rocky earth, silt sediments, bleak leftover mineral woodland sands, such gifts of glaciers. The generation of settlers who, initially, had taken off its massive trees. The two roads connected, as one looping road, up and down, bearing wagons, horse and rider. The trees have, of course, reseeded themselves.

Personal Recreation

God makes the personal and the impersonal. Sometimes we can believe in the first concept and not the second . . . and these swap positions, back and forth in the belief "system" of a person. The personal aspect would mean that God relates to us, personally. Otherwise God would not make the personal, not make persons.

Sometimes I have almost no sympathy with angels, and vice-versa. Were you to see one in its barest visible form it would look more like a mathematical equation than a person—or *any being* we might *recognize*. C.S. Lewis got this right in his science fiction, *Perelandra*. They are abstractions but we may say their bodies, if ever visible, are lightning, the earth and moon in tension, circulation of blood, the relative velocity of motion, the lack of our special pleading that *up* might be *down* and down up; a broken bone. An angel a broken bone?—But they've got a job to do and they don't really care much about us.

Until this happened I had thought angels were beings of the calculus, of light—austere, mathematical, impersonal burning charity. Charged with the earth, with the solar system, with planes of design and invention. But I wasn't thinking of them now. I was busy driving myself to boredom—work work work multi-task, e-mail e-mail e-mail; I had no time for Your Sabbath, through which all is finished, done.

It was a day like any other, the great Angel turning giant Earth, so that its shadow-line between light and dark was momently compassing a circuit across the mighty sphere, day now chasing night across the salt-wet expanse far far away; touching almost simultaneously the summits of the great central Maine Mt. Katahdin and coastal Mount Desert. I did not consider it. I was near the bottom of a steep rugged lane in the Western Mountains of Maine, preparing my bike, removing its dew-stained covering, hitching my water bottle to its frame. My plan was to go meet the God of beginnings, devotionally, before returning to begin the day's work.

It was routine. I was bored in routine, even as God was remaking all things, out of nothing, with equations, with words.

I rolled down through the sand, which had gathered at the bottom of our lane in obedience to the principal of erosion. The momentary instability posed no problem for me on these fat tires that aid what little skill I have on shifting terrain. I was off down the shaft of this valley, riding toward the north pond at the base of our road, still in shadow—a twilight of mountains' mist—until the great head of Helios could find and penetrate the dewy green shaft of this valley in its turning toward the light. I would return inadvertently that way again in a few days, bodily changed, sans bicycle.

I did half the circuit of the gleaming pond (packed with life and laws of the living). Leaves were tired green, loosing life, getting ready to color, then drop to earth. and now I was in the quiet thick of it, brambles on the power-line between that ledge high above and the south pond glimmering through thickets on my right. According to some psychic cum physical law, I was coming to life again myself, the dry bones of routine now animated in this special place. (Oh throw me into that briar patch.)

Not a whole lot of blackberries here. I went up and down in the secrets of this place and dragged my bike through knocked down leavings of loggers, through the gravel pit of a new developer, then swung out on the dirt road; passing down the lane toward the third pond. I was cautious on the downhill, not moving fast, knowing the territory, expecting jack-in-a-box dog to come ripping out of its yard, against the municipal law. Putting his master in defiance of it. (What George MacDonald analogy do I often use?—"We don't break the laws, we break ourselves upon the laws.") When it happened I halted and called out to them, knowing they'd never answer but just leave me to my task of conscience, duly rendered. Then I went on my way. I had better luck on the next hill, finding, at the tip end of the season, enough blackberries to satisfy—a lean year it's been for berries, my neighbors agree.

This was a day fit only for the work of angels, severe beings of principle and law, and light over the pattern—over the warp and will of mitochondria and gametes endlessly weaving eternity down into bottomless life; in smaller constituents, back out again to the furthest body of light or dark matter—that look back toward the first reach of space and time.

Now I would reach the far point in this morning's routine bike ride from home; begin drifting downhill back toward the opposite shore of the south pond, off the dirt road. On the macadam, sampling the view as it shone blue through gaps in trees. Oh, just one last stop, just one or two more handfuls of blackberries, and I would get on with the work of the day. I was rounding that curve of the incline, just a bit weary, awkwardly dismounting man's bike with crossbar, in order to walk it up.

But I could feel the laws pulling on me as I did so: a crossbar, my seat too high for the length of my stride, the angle too obtuse for my foot to gain purchase, gravity here as anywhere; the ancient rock just below me formed and hardened in the deeps of earth and pushed up again by forces of erosion and frost-wedging. The measure and weight of my own bones formed of mineral materials—but still not hard enough to compete with granite formed in the crucible of fire and geologic time.

I lay on a small knoll in gravel off the curving shoulder, my bike lying above me just off the macadam. I rolled over on my side to get away from bright pain. I stared out at the pond's blue chop between tall red trunks of pine. And there, across the pond, was the hill with power line that I had traversed . . . and blue sky above branches, Helios in the trees, red-pine needles shielding me.

I thought: *I'm not bored.*

This, I am bound, is an *adventure*. Not the one I had hoped for three weeks down the road. The one where we would be flying first-class for only $100 a seat, all told, to Edinburgh Scotland and a castle that Allen has wanted me to see. (Our son, J.D. loads baggage for a living just now, hence the cheap fare.) That was not going to be boring . . . And I saw that this also was not going to be boring . . . but in a different way.

I hear the rumble and whoosh of a car coming around this curve above me and turn my head for a phantasmal peripheral view of its passing. And then another . . . and then both are stopping for me, I suppose. Lying still, resting as well as one might—given the pain—I hear a tentative voice speaking . . . something impersonal:

" . . . I see a woman lying there, and her bicycle . . . Do you suppose she needs help . . . ?

I'm lying here deciding whether or not to say anything. I feel there is all the time in the world and God watching me.

". . . help . . ." It's a small offering.

And now he's standing fore off the port bow of this rudderless crate, with an air of speculative inspection. I'm wiggling my toes and testing other skeletal features, upper body, neck, fingers and arms.

He's somewhat stocky; he wears a baseball cap. ". . . Is there something I can do for you . . . ?"

"I need an ambulance, sir." I tend to turn martial in such situations.

He's gone from my line of sight, presumably back to his car and 911 on the cellphone . . . Now there are two of them talking somewhere above me. It's a conference about how the one has to go to work and the other has only to go to Rumford.

?

It's all set then, the driver of the second car will remain until the ambulance comes. A woman, by her voice. The man apologizes for leaving, but somehow I peel some sort of story out of him before he goes. He'd been in an accident, not too dissimilar from this, broken bones, but the extra spice to his pain was that he had to crawl up out of water onto the shore. *Goodbye, and thank you.*

The voice that had been speaking behind me moved around the wrecked crate and stood before me in the form of a short boxy woman dressed in casual blue, shorts and matching top, I think . . . her form but an impression . . . for I was lying on my side looking up where she stood—off away under the pines between me and the pond.

I had ceased testing my members and knew the exact residence of pain . . . though I found out later that it differed from the broken thing in me needing repair. I lay on my left side propped on an elbow, my right leg against my left to ease the bright pain. It was proper to be sociable and respectful toward my helper, so I propped myself with the flat of my left hand, trembling, holding my torso upright in the gravel while making conversation.

There followed meandering talk having little to do with our little predicament. I did learn that Terry had once suffered a broken leg.

I said, "I landed hard on my hip and thought that was what broke, but now I'm sure it's my leg, the thigh bone. Definitely broken."

We talked a bit about her St. Bernard, a huge rescuing animal. And of course, being a writer, I made the mental analogy and moved on. Terry offered to call a family member on her cell phone . . . I think this was after she picked up my bike and locked it to one of the pines. I tried to think of Allen's number at work: what came to mind was that of my son living in the next town. While they conversed I lay, still propped on an elbow and shaky right hand, listening. Listening for the sound of a siren. Terry and I talked on. Did I pray out loud for her and her family? I'm pretty sure I asked for God's blessing on them. It was a strange thing to do lying there in the dirt on the side of a knoll between a mountain and the pond. I'm sure neither of us expected it.

A tiny sound at first, far away, disembodied sound moving through hills and trees, past pond-side retreats. It moved according with moral law, municipal law, and grand implacable laws of physics. I knew that my name was in that sound, I had not once doubted that it would be. I had all the time in the world, and with Terry there for company, I wasn't uninterested. Now it resonated in the delicate bones of my ears like the great shrieking monster it would've been thought in a land far away—on this exact shore— but 150 or 200 years ago. Had I hurt myself then, whose sole job would it be to sit in an office with electronic equipment receiving calls for aid of every stripe from tiny electronic handhelds sending messages through the air? Who so quick and knowledgeable to traverse the hills in a swift, blinking, wailing, little emergency room on wheels—a thing unknown in those days? What would have become of someone like me trapped in bright pain, broken on a rock?

But I love those days. I hold them in my imagination almost constantly.

I think the prayer I made for Terry increased in value when she heard the scream as they lifted me onto the gurney. They had introduced themselves but I had forgotten their names. Terry insisted on staying with them until they could secure the old crate and get it onboard. I heard her say to somebody that my hip was broken, whether to my son or the EMTs, I don't remember . . . only I was certain she had made a mistake. It was my leg, the femur, strongest bone in one's body.

The ambulance completed the circuit of south pond for me, carrying broken cargo, rattling and swaying, my neck in a collar, my body in traction; the man slitting my jeans on an outside seam, slitting the sleeve of my blouse for the IV; cranking my leg up another notch, and me responding to all his questions with the martially appended "sir." I had been trussed like a mummy going into a gleaming tomb, a brand-new ambulance, I think he said it was new. My body temperature plummeted and I shivered, shivering-shivering-shivering, and the man was saying, "My name is Craig, call me Craig, don't call me sir."

"You look like my brother," I said as he bent over me, cheeks jowly, mustache salt-and-pepper, the obligatory ball cap—was he balding like my brother? "In Ohio."

"I've got a brother in Ohio, too."

Swift as a magician he flung a toasty coverlet over me.

The moving emergency room jiggled, squeaked and screamed through the hills I could not see; its hurt person swaying rhythmically past hamlets, only the apexes of gables flashing clear morning light reflected from high windows into the burnished sides of my tomb. I was fascinated by those perfect small triangles moving past, the topmost of houses inhabited by strangers, my neighbors in these rural communities dotting the hills on our shrieking twenty-five mile route to the county seat.

"Norm," he said, as we passed through the roadway construction zone filled with workers, heavy equipment and cars, "that siren's too loud."

Craig was working somewhere up above me, monitoring my vitals and alternately speaking to the hospital emergency room of my condition. As he swung into view above me I noticed the sweat running rivulets on his face while below I was complaining of the cold, my teeth chattering. "Shock," he said. I would have to remember to thank him for this, I thought, and then I was thanking him . . . just in case I forgot when we arrived at port outside the emergency room.

We stopped and doors were opening, an angel's face flying by, his white hair afloat in the breeze, voice subdued with courage and brokenness: "I'm here sweetheart." And me laughing, saying, "How'd you do that!"

How did you get here ahead of me? Did you fly forty miles?

Somebody made a joke about the quality of the ambulance ride. Was it me? There had been another great scream, but now I was being rolled on a gurney without my trusses, without the stabilizing traction and collar of the EMTs. What were they doing?—couldn't they see I needed that stuff?! Surely it's all about *me*? But I said, sincerely, and largely to correct any impression of ingratitude, "I thought angels were great beings of light . . . Turns out they're fat men with mustaches and baseball caps."

I recall thinking, They are female, black and wear glasses, they are dumpy and white, know what to do with broken people rolling on gurneys down to x-ray. Gossiping, ignoring me, they were talking about the quality and kind of food in restaurants in Maine, the prices, et cetera. It's what I've suspected all along: there's no comparison between what they do with food here and what they do down South.

They didn't seem to be thinking much of my comfort (it's all about *me*), but at least they knew what to *do with me*. Continually I thought of what they should do *for* me, but the only *truth* given was their doing as they did. Oh these people so wise and good, so just-doing-their-jobs, angelic.

After the metallic—metallic and glass?—slab, and the photographs and the turning this way and that, the being carefully lifted and placed on a movable bed, the howling—I remember a strong desire not to be moved after that . . . hearing a reassurance that I'd be staying, with the drip of morphine for awhile, on this bed. This blessed bed on which they were rolling me . . . Where was it they were rolling me?

"We are going to do a partial hip replacement." A middle-aged man, with mustache and glasses whose name I could not pronounce, was saying this. Its prefix was Dr., of the orthopedic variety, so it didn't matter to me personally, except I did not want to offend him by mispronouncing it. My best approximation was that if I put a grr sound in front of a Ramsey, I'd be okay. Allen was with me and this surgeon was explaining things. I liked the fact that he seemed to want input from us, but the true and joint desire of my spouse and I was for him to do what he knew best.

The anesthesiologist explained the options for us, but of course we decided to go with what she knew to be best, the saddle-block. I was not going to go deep, but I was going to go painless. Besides, I was interested in the O.R. experience. Wouldn't it be neat if I could watch while they put in the new hip-joint ball? Just think, a new part for my body was on its way up from Portland. What did this say about life in general?

Things are not as clear here as I thought they would to be. I can see bright lights between a crack in the blue blanket placed over my head, I can hear continual conversation that makes no sense in what seems like a roomful of busy workers—and there's a continual disembodied hammering—something that sounds an impersonal *knock-knock*. Yes, I think he's got to hammer some holes to secure my new ball-joint, but what's that strange music they're playing?

It's the musical equivalent of the jiggling, swaying and squeaking ambulance ride. The highway is under construction. We are driving madly through the hills trying to escape the revenuers at warp speed . . .

For many days afterward I will try to puzzle it out. Was it a sort of bluegrass rap music, jitterbug hoedown? To say it was manic would be to downgrade mania to a sedate walk in the park. But of course that irrational music may have been only my mind at play . . . but I think not. It elevated the whole experience into the realm of artistic creation, and that's why I suspect God was doing the creating while I drifted on for fifteen minutes admiring God's handiwork. This must be in some fashion how angels work. How can we comprehend the layers and levels of their sub-creating beneath the mighty power of God?

Can I tell you how disappointed I was to learn that my fifteen minutes had been, by the clock, an hour-and-a-half? Or that I experienced an hour-and-a-half as fifteen minutes: I was not bored.

Those workers were busy roundabout me, and for me, in the impersonal manner of construction workers remaking a stretch of highway, careful in their craftsmanship and use of heavy equipment. Continually thinking of safe operation, regulated flow of traffic through the work area, putting up with irritants of dust and heat or rain and wind, snow. Always a care for the work, but nary a thought for the ground beneath the graded surface, beneath steamroller, hot-top paving machine, or snowplow. Yet those in the O.R. were just doing their jobs in what seemed to me a highly creative atmosphere. The workers into whose care I awoke were as busy but, in tension different from those of the O.R. Though you will find many of the same workers there from time to time. The difference, I suppose, is the personal, as opposed to the impersonal, creative.

In my experience creative work is impersonal, requiring craft. Craft does not seem to belong to the personal sphere, where it descends to the manipulative. Yet, the personal is where spontaneity rules . . . as it only *appears* so in art. Craft in creative work may also be guided by the moral law, the Tao. But what could be more creative than spontaneity? Personal and impersonal, it is God working in both law and in wild spontaneity.

I cannot do justice to the world of the hospital floor with its kind smiling helpful shifting inhabitants, perpetually busy on behalf of those who are little able to do for themselves. Here I rediscovered self-knowledge. These workers must attend personally, face-to-face, in a spirit of warm courtesy, kindness, knowledge—and a care-giving that comes from submitting in some measure to empathy with another's bodily ills. How can this spirit be so constantly smiling, friendly and kind? What a world is here: everyone cares. Stephens Memorial Hospital is almost as much like the world as God had in mind. How nice for God to have found willing workers. How relaxing for God to take a break from dealing with and harmonizing the crazy, chaotic, misfit, and frequently evil, element. God's work must be done here.

That seemingly sterile place, always florescent-lit, is a walk in the cool of the evening in paradise for God. From my first to last personal encounter since the rock in the road, every caregiver I spoke with (if I remember right Craig and Norm included) had been hurt, injured, or endured disease: the tear-down-the-house, rip-out-the-foundation, take-it-to-the-ground work of devils and angels. Somebody's working on us, and there are times when I peripherally note ourselves collaborating in the work of angels. There are times in your life when you can only see something from the corner of your eye. It disappears when you try to look at it dead on. Like stars of such scant magnitude vanishing in the night when looked at directly. Who knows but that they are the mightiest galaxies, if furthest away in space and time?

I saw many deeply personal things about myself and others, about those I love and those I scarcely experienced: mighty things. I thought seeing had power enough to change me. But, except for what feels like an 8-ball in my hip pocket, I am unchanged, the same ornery little potato I was born. Created, that is—with plenty of room to make all the mistakes I cared to, every one of which has my own personal name in it, sometimes shrieking. I could feel those laws pulling on me as I dismounted that bike with crossbar. Time stretched. It seemed there had been all the time in the world to stop. *Yes, my mind was thinking, You could put the brakes on this parabolic flight, this fall. You needn't dismount on this incline with that crossbar, the seat so high.*

I rarely notice how gentle and accommodating my spouse is, how generous and willing to go far for me. A pilot. True pilot. After a few days he drove me home from the strange wonderful magic place that is Stephens Memorial Hospital with its dedicated workers, its generous do-the-job-without-stint workers. We took the same highway through hills back toward the valley of the ponds, and there we encountered highway workers still ditching, smoothing, crowning, paving; that long stretch between the two great hills.

If you have never read Anne Morrow Lindbergh's *The Steep Ascent*, you might read for its troubling atmospheric adventure, pioneering a path among the confusing alpine peaks; read for her literary workmanship. After the steep ascent, in a craft of the early days of aviation exploration, there followed the steep *descent*—in regular order. And when she and her pilot spouse got down from those skies over the Alps in their fragile craft, she was struck by the undying atmospheres, laws, principles, levels and layers of impersonal holy bright and burning love. The thing I am walking in, am writing and speaking in.

I'm looking out my window watching the workers as Allen drives me through that construction zone. Moving earth, setting directional cones, laying pavement, directing traffic, talking on handhelds. All just doing their jobs, getting paid, in the spirit of how You want.

Things done in hiding, mighty things. How You created everything out of Your Word.

Toward Big Winter

October

This a.m., almost first thing, we cleaned the stove pipe. It's a soapstone stove with catalytic combustor, but ash and creosote accrete, need brushing out once a year. He stands on the roof with long handled brush, I'm in our house, beside the stove hugging a plastic trash bag round the stovepipe— precaution against Ashy House Syndrome . . . Next, he's replacing the com- bustor—does this every five years. We heat the house with this woodstove and locally cut firewood. The pipe-and-stove cleanout is frustrating work. Every step along the way something goes wrong. While he works, tools clinking, I gaze at the cold ash dust drifting up the stovepipe on a draft between woodstove and pipe.

We are a member of the creation story. It's not easy to get my head around it, or my keyboard for that matter, but I think God pays people to read God's story. It's the reverse of the commercial mind. God makes parts of the living story capable of "reading" it themselves, through the experi- ence of *being*—human being—in His story. God gives breath and body and situation—*Being*—to the story-parts interesting to him . . . Not only is God telling the story, sort of seeming from outside in the gallery (as it were), but God is the story being told in time and throughout time, and we are some of its parts. (Clear?) Anyway, see where the "pay" comes in? We get all the good gifts of *being* in exchange for reading the story . . . but, yes, *we* pay to be part of, as well as to read, the story. That's where evil comes in. The evil part of God's *Gift of Being*. The ashy house syndrome. In this telling evil means *suffering*. Not the bad we *do*, per se, but the *suffering* it causes.

The screwy thing about all this is The Self. In the beginning Self came in with all the fairy godmothers, and Self (who looks a bit like Gollum) says to God, "You wouldn't be having all this without paying your worshipers. If you stopped paying them with only good gifts they would cease to 'believe.'" (Can you see Gollum making scare quotes with grasping, boney, spindle fingers?)

God looks into the account balances of creation, sees some leftover energy from the beginning, and says, "Well here's some power leftover from my initial struggle to get it all going (without that it wouldn't go): Pure Suffering . . . See what you can do with that. But I don't think it will work out as you want."

"Why not?"

(Pause)

God gives no answer.

(For the moment.)

My Ghost on His Periphery

Here's an account of a youth seeing my ghost in these woods and being scared out of his mind. You may say, she exaggerates.—Out of his mind? You may say, How can someone see your ghost when you are still in the body, alive?

That's a mystery to me too. Let's see if I can unravel it here. I love to go into the woods at any time, day or night, whether on snowshoes, hiking or biking. Maine woods at night have an entirely different quality. Depending on clouds and phases, moonlight shafts down through black boles, producing crossing-hatchings and mysterious patterns everywhere. But you have to be careful about woods-walking around here, especially during deer season when apparently, under certain conditions, it may be legal to shoot me (as deer) between dawn and dusk.

However, because All Hallows Eve was approaching, this particular haunting happened during bird-hunting season. It was still dark, I was in woods on a track, walking toward a pond-side road leading to the highway and that all-important cup of coffee. Distantly I heard the start-up of a two—or was it a four?—stroke engine; an all terrain vehicle, or ATV. Probably a four-wheeler. This, maybe, was one of the teenagers living by the north pond a quarter-mile away through dark woods.

This time of year, as we verge on winter, leaves are scarce except when deep, crunching, underfoot. This particular track is varied, sometimes winding along the brook, sometimes curving beneath a wooded knoll, solitary and tree-crowded in the dark.

I began to wonder about the engine-revving teenager. Maybe he'd take this pathway on one leg of his (I supposed) woodland journey toward school? He was making an irritating end-of-night racket—enough to wake the proverbial dead. (The dead are but proverbs.)—Distant. Yet listening now, I was fairly sure . . . the ATV was headed this way.

I admit to being (perhaps willfully?) secretive. Liking to hike and hide, slipping unnoticed away (if possible). But this was bound to be tricky as well. Two things: The trail was rocky. I did not want to startle him on the machine in this dark. And I really did not want him to think he had a crazy old neighbor lady woods-walking trails in the dark; or some other creature in his headlights. He was coming. A glow of light shone over a crest thronged with tall trunks to either side of the trail. Leaves crunching, acorns rolling underfoot, I stepped off among trees. Had to step over a blowdown or two, steady myself, arm out, hand clasping a tall sapling. For added adventure I made what seemed an instinctive decision to stand perfectly still. (Like a deer.) I thought maybe he'd bucket past without notice. He would not be going super fast, but rockiness makes for bucking anyhow. I was in the trees.

Slowly now. There he goes, lights leading along the pathway. Passing, kinda standing (in his stirrups so to speak). Lithe, dressed for class. The backpack.

He's past.

Only my eyes moved, watching him. I'm standing still, arm out, hand on the tree.

It must've been peripheral vision. That's all I can think. Though I never moved, from the corner of his eye, he had caught the ghostly, standing in woods. Turned his head around to make sure, yelped, gunned it and flew off, screaming. *Screaming.*

That screaming was totally unexpected. First thing I thought—abstractly—was, Hope you don't get thrown onto the rocky trail. Into the woods. Hope you are rider enough to control that trajectory. Hope. Hope. Etc.. Etc.. *Then* I moved.

Surprised, yes. I don't remember laughing. Maybe I should have?

Have you ever noticed, on a starry night, that some stars are invisible to the direct gaze? The young man might have seen me almost directly in his headlights, through the trees, on his way along the curving trail. But he didn't notice me until it was *actually too late to see.* That would be the puzzle, were it not that some stars are visible solely with peripheral vision: If you look directly at these much lesser magnitudes stars, you miss them altogether. They are invisible to the human eye. There—but as ghosts in the Mind of God, ghosts on your periphery.

Guess I'm not a crazy old lady after all. Guess I'm a ghost. Yes. That's it. My ghost that still lives in this body was visible on his periphery . . . .But . . . evidently, in turning to confirm, he saw my flesh-clothed ghost *directly* as well.

So my theory must be flawed.

That coffee sure tasted good when I reached my lighted destination on the highway. I had too much of a good time recounting that episode across the counter. To the young waitress not much older than the school boy, with a much kinder heart (than mine). She inadvertently shamed me when sincerely hoping he did not come to harm.

I think he *was* unhurt, however. Because I heard him screaming the length of the trail, screaming while crossing the cobbled stream, screaming remotely up the wooded pass all the way to the (locally so-called) Million-dollar house overlooking our valley of ponds.

And, it appears, I'm still rather heartless over it. Enough to tell about it here.

November 17, 2009, Thursday

"Take, eat, this is my body." That was yesterday after arrival in Camden. After the bookstore, after our hike up Mount Battie through a rocky November woodland brown with fallen leaves and running streams—treacherous footing on sneakers, the wrong shoes. Did not know I'd need my hiking boots.

We had hiking sticks however and Allen helped me over the rough. Windy up through, and down and up, and the sky a shouting blue, and we arrived at the top with its "castle" after a bit of coaxing—on my part.

The last quarter mile was steepest but easier walking—it was a road!

I climbed the old stone tower. *Oh the view.* Penobscot Bay Islands: And this is but a small part of The Gulf with its 4,000 islands and indented coasts that, with indentations removed, might be laid across the continent stem to stern. Camden below and tiny, kinda dear even though I don't know the place much. Mount Battie is but a big rock! Edna St. Vincent Millay's rock. Pictures with the Lieca. *The wind.*

Allen was getting chilled and there was the walk down through the wind, but this time on the road. Very steep in spots and I took them backward—easier on the knees, feet and tendons.

Drive to The Ledges on Route 1 past Camden, Rockport. Room with a view, direct, of the Bay very deserted—Glen Cove—the curving white line of tidal approach. Brief rest (we'd also walked a bit of the Public Landing—more pictures). Then the brief drive into Rockland.

BOOKSTORES!

Rock and Book Cafe browsing. Buy my first Chandler, *The Lady In The Lake.* Also a Henry James I've not read before—*The Reverberator*—never even heard of it, and what a strange title for James. Used. Both for under nine dollars—expensive but this is the tourism coast of Maine.

And the walk down Main Street.

And then.

The *Offshore Restaurant.* This noticed on our way and recommended by The Ledges' clerk. Closed when we pulled in. One car. Dark interior, sign said open Tuesday through Sunday (it was now Monday). Allen comes back, says, "They're experimenting—it's open." And in we go.

Cap of the day. We sat watching the light, sky-leaving. Going. There was the roadway and its passing cars I did not much notice.—Across the way beyond them . . . The filigree of great multitudinous twigs and branches against the sky. What food, seafood and salad, but first the Belfast Lobster Ale—surprise. And I kept watching, Staring at that great delicate tracery of multitudinous twigs and branches against a not-quite-darker sky. And then I noticed it, watching, the cross. Upholding great lines of power. I saw the dark rugged cross in among this great dark spread and complex design of limbs and twigs.

And we talked, and I kept watching as it become more pronounced. Noting changes, its brutishness and power, in the dim light-leaving sky. Growing greater in strength, angularity, ruggedness and brutality there in that deep design.

Below, behind, was a shadowy house, a home hospitable, lit on either side of its front doorway. And a few shadows of people going in and out. And it is all here, and all Your doing . . . and we are along for the ride, and to see *what* you're doing. Glimpse what it *cost* you. Suffering—pain and death. Death as yet but glimpsed by us here on the coast in these living makings, doings of Yours. Thank you.

December

December 6, 2009, Sunday

SNOWING LAST NIGHT AS Allen grilled steak on the porch with our small iron-dome grille. I saw flakes streaming through house-light as I walked up our steep drive from the mailbox, letters in hand. And I thought of the star-sprinkling seen the night before, looking out past branches and into that great bright-dark hole parted in the woods by our house itself. Last night snow fell like stars above the house. I had looked back at Allen then—silver-haired with ponytail—standing in our backyard in house-light. Then I glanced back up at those stars. I wondered if it were time to start again the winter book—*Maine Metaphor*—begun maybe 20 years ago and largely abandoned. Abandoned after "Winter Gains and Loss."

Monday, December 7, 2009

The Infamous Day. Feeling old and with related trepidations over winter—the season now upon us with uneasy footing. Literal uneasy footing. I had to force myself onto the road today. Imagination could not get motivation going inside the being . . . just shrinking from thoughts of darkness, the ice, the dogs, the cane, the shading . . . Until at last I might find myself in starry dark on our icy roadway flashlight in hand, looking for slick patches. Safely past the leaseless dog-walking neighbor. So—instead—Allen brought me to the bottom of the hill and let me out to go on my way, four miles there and back for coffee.

I tell myself, and it is true, I'd rather be lying in the road than whole and safe at home, warm but restless and unliving. When you get back home you are grateful to be home and warm. No longer restive and unliving.

I am old, past 60, and my confidence and flexibility, surefootedness and swift reaction—gone, or leaving.

It's dark out here, icy on this pavement. Road shoulders in darkness are crunchy and whitish, edged in stiff sand and adjacent icy patches on pavement. Brights of cars go past, my sleeve reflectors catching light. These roads are narrow, curving through hills. Words don't come so easy now. They bunch in awkward constructions. I'm a laggard, my mind hangs back. I fail to search out the right word. I care too little, feel deep reluctance, want to stop . . . but would meet my enemies, the restive unliving aspects of my being. I want to be alive . . . as long as I must be alive. I hope to be most alive when I am dead and gone from upper Earth.

This is the winter I've not looked for. I looked for adulthood, for maturity . . . but not this. This is the slow decay, the withdrawing of God's verve—as God wills—from the form. It's spotty—as though in withdrawing he makes his empty spaces wider, wider. I cannot bridge them with will. Even will now has its gaping spaces.

I'm sitting on the couch . . . our home given ten years ago, a heating pad at my back—making this black ink pen go through its motions. So afraid of disappointing God and by extension myself for not going on . . . Or is it the reverse, God loosing me? Do we swap places, God and I? When do I get to see Him?

And I used the cane to help me get to Round Pond Corner Store (Formerly Bob's welcoming Corner Store and Texaco) . . . looking, through extended darkness, on pools of disturbing light. Negotiating ice, circumscribing streaks and patches.

Afternoon after work. Reading *The Last Algonquin*, crying. The author but tells it at secondhand, out of his father's real experience with the last Bronx Indian. Joe Two Trees befriended him as a 10-year-old boy, the old man desiring to tell him his story so that it would not die when he went to the Great Spirit. And be remembered: Tchi-Manitou, Maker of All Things, "is very strict about the telling of stories." They must be told only in winter so as not to disturb preparations for winter in other seasons. For it is the maker's purpose to have his people ready for the hard season, the season when they might justly profit from stories. It has been a long time since I cried while reading a book. It is like the trail of tears—but one alone, a 15 year-old boy—the last of family, clan, and tribe.

Wednesday, December 9, 2009

Cloud blanket, but waning, still-pale moon visible as spot of moon-pale-light above—me standing, sipping coffee in the snowy yard between trees. Pale spot crisscrossed, snared in tapestry of dark branches. Now I've ruined my plan to put in red my *thoughts*—as opposed to the *experience* of winter. In red ink I have:

Suppose God made free will (past tense here—but need not be). But an opposition of his own will. Just bent, wearing long red underwear with horns and pitchfork delighting to provoke, evoke, invoke . . . hmmm . . . ? "Before" all was gentle courtesy, kindness, sweetness, light? Was God thinking, I don't want too much control so I'll make free will? Was this in tandem with the violence which brought all into being: That first act extrapolating, as his wont, into precision minutia of making, principles, mathematical, sub-particulate, atomic? And then he liked the idea of using leftover violence and power—lending violence and power to free will. Free will is a made thing, letting it loose to show what it would do . . . But not quite free? *Not free from restraint of consequence.*

. . . Speculating, standing in snow.

The *Flatland* book by Edwin Abbott is a bit hilarious on the i-pod—such a dry presentation, Mr. Edwin Abbott's. Why don't I care much for *dry*? Dry wit? I guess I like a friendly mockery but one with fond-feeling. Recognizable when you're not "smart person." I began listening in the dark road—the Gore—all my way back after I finished off my coffee from Round Pond Corner Store. *Flatland* seeming cold, uncaring, in dry wit.

Back to black ink:

Snowing out my window, full, gentle, soft. Gaze at it falling. My old friend. Greet my old friend—for the first time again. Infinity is like mooreeffoc. I think of my dream: snow-bathing with my hands, life in branches, *feeling* eternal life with my hands. This is God's broken body, falling in flakes of careful design. All things are made by him and nothing made without him.

Fall. Fall. Snow, you are what is. I will not dread your winter.

Thursday, December 10, 2009

The first real snowfall—six to ten inches. It's the a.m. and dark out. I've stepped out with coffee, standing just under an overhang to look up the hill direct, at countless snowy trunks. Everything in thick cover. Oh, the conifers wear it well, those soft triangular sloping bodies, very dim, yet the brightest thing going. As though standing patient, arms hanging, beneath the fresh cold burden upon them. Rank upon rank up the hillside. Everything is human to me . . . sometimes. The ultimate practitioner of the "pathetic fallacy."

Back to red ink (how much longer will I keep this up?):

The most daunting aspect of "life, the universe, and everything" [this part in red] is the *personal*. Look at the word—rooted in the word *person*. Creation is a massive achievement, unfathomable by the ordinary person. The physicist begins, however, the theoretical physicist. But the further into it he or she goes, the more he or she realizes how little there is for God to work with. And yet . . . there is so much of everything that we cannot get to the bottom of a cuticle on a fingertip. However great our magnification we will continually see more and yet more of strange . . . bits and pieces of you. And yet you are made up mostly of invisibility; that is, what appears to be more, and yet more, empty space. Nothing. In other words, it does not appear. I believe that God made/makes the world and everything—by faith. (Question aside: What would happen if God stopped believing?—All this nothing and all this everything together, by faith. It makes me want to encourage God. Give God moral support.) And thus, while tinkering with subatomic particles, and ever thinking about that and about the next move—in the back of God's mind, so to speak, maybe over there in that cloud of the horse nebula while on vacation after the initial lonely and painful effort—in the back of God's mind was the idea of *the personal*. The person. Person reading this. You. In particular.

Believe me: the Angels are inhuman. They are principles powers dominions formulas unbreakable laws. It's a stretch for any one of them to clothe in the semblance of a person. It's been done but it's not the usual thing. We go safe down the highway because of them. Because things are put together right, from the subatomic quarkiness to the brake job your mechanic did on your Toyota last month. Everything follows the rules and that's why there are no accidents.

. . . Um. (Naturally you are not reading this as you drive?)

Anyway. The hardest part is the personal. Because we are not exactly law-abiding even though our abode is the Land of Law . . . The law-abiding universe. There's that really irrational part called free will. Which means there's a certain amount of leeway to break the law.—Which George Mac-Donald asserted is not really the case; but that we break ourselves upon the laws. Yes, you can carbon-load the atmosphere all you want but then you'll get climate change, coughing and wheezing, greenhouse gas magnifying itself, not going anywhere anytime soon—with a whole lot of denial. You can, as Simone Weil said, turn a human being into a *thing* with killing. But then . . . you've got the one you have killed lodged in your conscience. It's that moral aspect that makes human, makes a person. And maybe this is what interests God so.

Is God Morality?

God is Light. In God is no darkness, no immorality. Light in coordination with my eyes gives me the ability to see. What is morality? Morality gives us safe bridges, safe cars, safe foods, safe medical help, etc.. Immorality makes everything unsafe. If workers and managers aren't morally stewarding their work, their jobs, corruption results. If a worker is incompetent, it's the manager's job to know and correct.

But this is total digression. I started out to write about the difficult feat, more difficult than the design of shining messengers of law. Harder than all-in-a-singularity, more difficult by far than evolution via mutation. Harder even than the apparent and careful knitting together of baby: "Meiosis, gametes, fertilization, zygote. Two cells, four cells, eight cells, *morula. Blastula, gastrula, embryo, fetus.* Baby." No, the hardest part is making a person. Part of which is the individual unique persona.

Making the personal also interests God because God is a Person.—Who made us to have that relationship, one-on-one, with God. Look at the Genesis story . . . In the cool of evening the talk with God.

Is God mutable? We are told no. Perhaps God's body is, broken bread, slaughtered lamb. In the beginning was making and breaking of singularity, violent gifting of Light, of Time. Creation, we have seen, is complete mutability. But why would God make mutable bodies for his persons. Maybe God makes his people bodily because God is lonely? Because God wanted someone to play with, like any kid might? Because God is a Person, too?

(Man's immortality is not here addressed.)

Albeit a Person who knows exactly all the parts of your hangnails and what condition these parts are in. Because he wants to be able to talk as a person, and relate as a person, and hears and knows you and me as persons? This has to be the most difficult part for us to get. Daunting. Because God only came here once as a Human Person. And you're maybe thinking, But he's been gone 2000 years. How can we get together now?

But more, almost—wouldn't it be almost daunting from the standpoint of Divinity Itself? All that controlling power . . . But then stepping back . . . speaking if at all in a whisper? A horse nebula whisper. Relinquished control in this one small aspect, free will is limited by other considerations mentioned: physical laws of reality. [are these textual parts any good? could they be fixed? Maybe adding research, insight?]

There is another way to have that talk with God without a time machine (other than the one we're in at the present moment). But you have to get real quiet. Maybe be alone, kind of even a bit lonely. I don't think you'll hear a whisper, even, in this material realm. But you will hear. But you will know. Because you are interested. Want to. Remember that free will thing. Because God does not want to blast you with God's great Person, blast you with conversation, arguments for his existence . . . Unlike us, God has no self. Yet God *can* be responded to, invited . . .

Make some kind of move.

You would just know. Know that He's here with you. And you perceive him in spirit. An impress on your spirit. Because God is spiritual, spirit. Then, in truth, you perceive God. In *Person*.

Friday, December 11, 2009

Snowshoeing Davis Park to the dentist's office this fresh blowing, pine whispering a.m.. Think of emendations for the journal—out of mind now—hope they come back soon. A lonely track and afraid I did not give myself time. Don't like to keep them waiting, especially since that time I forgot nearly two years ago.

The trail now is virtually unbroken though drifted waves of the snowshoer told, from the day before. When all this started. We are in for it now. What kind of winter will it be? I do love to snowshoe though . . . once the inertia is got over, the "entropy walking backward."—as I've seen it put by an author somewhere.

Twas the season's first such exercise. Watching Allen drive off, me leaning against a plow-row struggling into webbed shoes . . . I thought, Good won't be so hard getting over that plow-row of inertia next time. And it was—easy enough.

Saturday, December 12, 2009

Feeling want and lack, and already cold out of bed, I put on my overcoat and went out on the deck. But few stars, foredawn coming. Stood by leaning on railing looking out, and expressing my need. Lack and need are different. Lack is negative, signifying an empty space. Need signifies *desire* to be filled—for some good purpose.

I heard the wind on a mountain, north. Just there, over my shoulder, high. It was 15° and the wind up there. I heard it in high pines. The wind dropped down, like a walk from higher to lower trees. It got big . . . because it is here now, down on this lower tier . . . and in these surrounding trees, and in bare branches over there, oaks. But now it turns and comes down, and then up slightly, up under my clothing, the night clothes and overcoat, flapping and twirling, very cold, moving. Friendly, fond.

And *then* it withdrew. I don't know where it went. Or where it came from, really. But I think it was the Maker of all these things, stars, dawn, trees, mountain, deck, clothing, person—acknowledging the other person's prayer.

Late in the day I went down into our basement and brought up a long-handle roof rake. I've been out pulling cold snow off edges of roofing—where I could reach. The roof is icing at its edge under that load. Though the snow load is not yet so very great. I found that the roof is higher than I remember from last time I did this job—many months ago, when the depth underfoot was four feet.

Sunday, December 13, 2009

Standing on the deck in overcoat, Corona, with lime and ice, in hand. Leaning back on the railing, looking up at dusky snowflakes, each drifting down.

Thinking of God's making these cold flaking bits of God's being, with gratitude sweet. So sweet this time.

My face and eyes upturned to enjoy the soft feeling, sometimes turning to glance up into snowy woods, up past the roof-edge against sky just a bit paler than the ascending snow. Multitudinous bits and pieces, falling falling. And .

. . . Feeling the stuff blinked away from my eyes . . . I remember the first time I got mad at God—almost before I could talk, listening to my brother tell me about snow God made and how good it was. Someone big was getting us ready to go out in it. We were excited, going to see the snow God made.

. . . Sixty plus years . . . rejoicing. So gentle and sweet this snow, blinking away, gentle face-touching. Snow.

Thursday, December 17, 2009

Got up at 3:45, coffee (Yuban), made a fire, took coffee on the deck beneath winter stars overhead and lower among bare branches. Three degrees Fahrenheit and a wind across our narrow valley, but high on the low mountain ridge—there—southeast but coming . . . It came over, found me cup in hand, playing cold across my face, drifting hair. The stars up there! The cloud-suggestions. Dusky puffs of smoke above dark roof outlines. The prayer, uneasy, distant, self-absorbed. Malingering. God. Love. Love. I want to love you. I don't. I want to love you. *You.*

It's You, the shooting Star! There and gone. *You.* You let me know!

I go back and, leverage the combustor, find a coffee pot in candlelight, a nightlight, really, in the wall. Go back outside.

"I'll turn every stone until I get home to you . . . day after day . . ."—Julian Lennon, posted today on lj-user coldhighmountai.

Friday, December 18, 2009

Allen up, in the dark, building fire, brewing coffee. He brings it to me in bed, I drink, get out—so cold. Fifty-three°in the room, 7° outside. Warmer than yesterday. Overcome the inertia. Get on the overcoat, go out on our snowy deck. The sky now is no color. No stars, not at all black. It shall be blue.

Wind yesterday on the close ridge opposite, in the southeast there—but. Below, on the further side one would feel it North, standing there on one's deck. Gusts are where they will.

I survey this visual surround. A dark tree line is a U-shape surrounding me up hill and down both sides of my house. "My" but in no way possessed by me. It, rather more possessing me. I'm just one of its parts. The treetop line is a bristling contour, up hill and down, u-shaped, three continuous sides. Wind is up there talking but also it comes down here momently, buffeting, then away. Out across the white patch of our neighbors (below)—then the opposite ridge, of the little vale. A valley of running streams under ice, an abundance of them for so tight and small a vale. It also is u-shaped and not—as with the deck tree-surround—a trick of perspective. From here I can't see the bowl-shape of the valley—but it is. And a dead-end as regards all but wings and shod climbing feet. I suppose you could do it barefoot, but I wouldn't want to.

The opposite valley wall is serrated, a contour in silhouette of conifer, most regular against a colorless sky. I hear voices below it across the way. Adults and kids, but a few, waiting the school bus. It's Friday after all, the one before Christmas.

And inside now I think about Julian Lennon's, cosmic song. I want to compare it to his dad's *Across the Universe* which I had always loved. Must go see if I can find it on youtube. YouTube—was not there—nonexistent—for the first part of this lonesome book. *When I went hunting with Seth.*

Ever notice, reader or writer, the vast difference between how one's story is *told* versus how one's story is *lived*? It is almost as though God's taste in stories seems to gloss the high points and is mostly comprised, instead, of detritus. I don't understand why God doesn't get bored. Take the reading of blogs. Example:

> *I woke and my nose was running, the flour made me cough as I stared at a polka dot ceiling thinking of that awful thing I said when it looked like it was not an omelet but a pancake on my plate*

*yesterday. How did I know she was looking my way?—Could see it in
her eye. And then I sighed and went to Rite Aid for Q-tips. Oh well.*

God must love this stuff—there's so much of it. We just don't realize
it, but we are the greatest story ever told. God is telling our story to that
great cloud of witnesses, who have gone on before, even as we are living it
with him. In the Space & Time he is evidently wearing. No one else could
bear the fathomless responsibility. That great witness of clouds. From all his
stories of that time past.

I plan no more online commenting.

Christmas Day, 2009

Standing on deck in the dark a.m., and listening to faint whumping of ice
on the pond more than half a mile remote, beyond many, many trees. The
ice is speaking, distantly bellowing, reporting on its expansion across and
beneath the pond's own expanse.

Later we walk down the snow lane where it all began for our friend.
Not too long a trek in the fresh winter air.—If you are carrying lumber as
he did more than once, getting new flooring in, to snug up the house. When
snow deepens all must be carried in arms, backpack, or on sled. There is the
sled track, on our right. I'm on the left, a foot path through snow over some
vehicle's track. Soon the only thing going here will be those on snowshoes
or snow machine, aside from wild critters. Skunk, which I smell on leaving
the car, fox, fishers, deer, moose. Any sane bear on this mountain will be
snoozing, living off the fat of the land (so to speak).

But we are carrying in Christmas goodies, either hand each, and expect to meet up with more such goodies yonder, beyond the solar electrified sheep fence, in our friend's snug house.

It is a simple green-stained house, narrow and tall with metal snow-
shedding roof. The main part had been built on piles—reinforced concrete
poured into sauna tubes . . . Before we thought better of living up here and
sold it to our friend for one dollar. He has done exceptional things with it
and learned exceptional things and will go on to doing so. Allen lifts up
the rusted bolt to lose the electrified gate and in we go, careful to close and
replace its makeshift latch.

Now I can smell sheep on the trail, sheep droppings beneath our feet
in this snow. I step off into snow next the trail. There's much less of it. Our
friend has done lots here and sometimes in roundabout ways with scraps of

this and that, with old-time machinery, photovoltaics (to power the fence) and a generator when needed for tools. The place is off the power grid and so requires continual labor for upkeep and to proceed—the stay against cosmic entropy ensues here, as everywhere. There are the sheep, colorful assortment, but five, with ram, horns thick and curling. Two white, one brown, and one black (lamb) ewes—and all look like small woolly barrels walking on dark small stick-like legs. *Maaaaa!*

I'm timid around the ram. He'll charge his own shepherd trying to get grain. He gets push back on that but it doesn't seem to stop him. Sometimes our friend gets fed up, locks him in and just tosses what the bullying ram needs over the fence . . . This brown ewe is a special concern now. She needs loving attention to get through winter, a dose of worming medicine and more grain, other. She and her black lamb had been staying close to the shepherd. Winter looks like it will be rigorous. Also he had a dream about an highly agitated polar bear tangled in the electric fence and attacking the brown ewe, who couldn't get away though she kept trying. He explained to me that the polar bear was, of course, not actual, but a symbol of brutal winter.

Inside the house is almost as utilitarian as the outside, but warm and comfortable with emblems of great beauty on its walls. Used to be the up-stairs was full of his carefully made sculptures. But most of these are on display elsewhere now—great gifts of a great heart to folk large and small. Beautifying the elsewhere and those minds and eyes gazing on them.

He looks over the food gifts to see what he can do with them in aid of our feast. We sit on the donated couch and watch him work with two kinds of cabbage—purple and savoy—a ham, cast-iron dutch oven; savory turkey and rutabaga chowder made with thyme, garlic and evaporated milk. Vinegar is one of his secrets for good cooking. Plum pudding (the homemade kind, dense as fruitcake) grilled with butter. The smell of wood smoke issuing out, he drops two great chunks of scarcely split wood into the firebox, stoking the oven to 400°. He's a tall man, slim, dark-haired, handsome, and will be 40 next year.

Soon we are donning our outdoor clothing again. This will be a bit of a working Christmas. He needs help penning the shed together for the brown and black ewes. We follow a narrow track winding around the fodder-feeding, inquiring sheep in corral fencing. We climb over a 2 x 4 threshold into a newly fenced-off space especially for the ailing, but now mending, ewe and her lamb.

Allen and I watch him shovel snow off pressure-treated plywood, which he has reinforced, for the roof. As he works he talks about the shaving files he's working with, mentioning as he does so how much safer they would be for a child being taught to carve or shape wood. Far safer than knives, with their fine blades.

Now they are holding the sidewall and roof together, our friend screwing them tight, screws going in at an angle for strength. He uses a power hand driver previously juice-up via the generator, and has just enough power to get walls and roof together before it gives out. The low shed is stable, strong, and firm when they get done. He's had the help needed from Allen, so can do the rest on his own tomorrow before the coming storm rushes into these Western Mountains of Maine.

And, best of all from stomach's point of view, the meal inside will be nearer ready now that some Time has elapsed, filled with the worthy work of others.

. . . Later, while waiting desert, we got talking and our friend told us about the question he was asked at work yesterday, Christmas Eve. "What's the meaning of life?"

His coworker asked for this answer of another and was told to ask our friend. He has a reputation for such considerations. But he had hesitated. He was about to answer when it occurred to him: What does "meaning" mean in this context? It came to him that "purpose" might be the better question.

He had brought me Mark Twain's *Roughing It* the other day. I asked him what he was reading now besides Kingsolver's *Prodigal Summer*. A sort of intro to *Little House on the Prairie* books . . . and he said therein was some information of how things were done on the domestic front, hints on how to live now off the grid and without fossil fuels, from an age gone by.

He is a little bit like God, Who puts in the supreme effort to bring and keep the universe in *being*; by his work here—by an ingenious combination of inception and extrapolation involving the transmutation of "this and that" and bits of everything into something else. Don't think the transubstantiation of bread and wine into the body of Christ is possible? Why do we eat, then, if the substance of what we eat does not make our bodies into—well, our bodies? Have you heard that we are made out of particles of stars? Have you read the Asimov science-fiction story in which the solar system of another galaxy was destroyed in fashioning a supernova worthy to signify and guide the Wise men into the heart of earth's Middle East. Where the Christ Child awaited their gifts: gold for a king, incense for God, myrrh, for his burial.

Saturday, December 26, 2009

On our way from Wal-Mart, humidifier balls secured for the winter, an idea came to me: I'd like some artists to accomplish a moving arts story of us. Beginning in thick darkness, then the quick glimmer and flash of singularity; through a big bang and beyond. Beyond. In the upheaval of particles—subatomic particles—and waves. Waves of light and dark matter/energy flowing and buckling and soundless exploding, pouring forth and drawing in, and pouring forth in profuse and copious violence, constantly changing and charging, making and remaking of all. So much is happening, and in time so tautly compressed, that it will require these artists shift focus to but one small seeming-mote of the whole uninterruptible flow of bright and dark matter (pouring without surcease into, and incorporating, the great basin of space). There, in that focal pin-point, that particle of fission/fusing elemental and making, the viewer is mesmerized and drawn near, by sheerest artistry, to a fixed attention. Our Mr. Sun is the local explosive angelic messenger of life, but one dimpling in brightness among an infinitude of such pulsing dimples in an outspreading garment of space-time—worn, but not in anyway containing, the Great One—the God of this making—Who Alone Is Worthy of such responsibility—such effort and deep design.

But it goes on from there, this visual, aural, sensual, and moral reenactment. Because, remember, I wanted it—and desired it—on coming away from that ugly, old big-box store. Be it the story of *us*. Earth. Before the great intermission that has not yet even made its appearance . . . although the stage has been set for it. Start small, after you have achieved Earth, my fellow artists, on your way to making us. Bypass all the cartoons of the amoeba and jellyfish and dolphins with legs. Go straight to the womb—forget the chicken and egg—show the depth of our making there in dark obscurity and you will have the most intricate part of the story . . . If you can really conceive every process, enfolding/unfolding, coding/decoding secrets—from these deeper darker parts of the earth.

Monday December 28, 2009

After a day of falling rain, "wintry-mix" and mountain streams flowing, I go out into starry darkness a.m. on the road where Allen has dropped me. He pulls away into the dark toward last days (hoped for) in the paper mill. Almost 20 years there; far longer than what was *then* hoped for. I wrote in my *Metaphor* pages—that seeming-generation ago—that I hoped to earn something through this action, this writing-down-words, enough to relieve him forever, with leftovers on which to fly.

Did not happen.

And here I am gingerly walking in slick darkness, beneath stars, by an expanse of tree-spangled *whump*-ing ice; walking deep down among dark serrate aisles of conifer, solely to turn upon inertia the expense of effort to outlive this life.

It's not easy. I'm old. I can barely creep over this stuff, stay out of cars' way rightfully going here by virtue of machinery. So what if I've a flash-light? Will that stop me—from causing accidents—of the sort that might conceivably ruin all these drivers' lives?

But I wanted to think! instead of this rubbish poured off in its firing of my brain's electrons and neurons . . . think instead of accreted accomplish-ment of our primitive, short-lived, struggling ancestors; on whose shoul-ders, whose bones, we so casually assume our comforts.

Allen, who began as an electrician, was demoted to papermaking for wearing "facial hair" (a beard), and later promoted to thermographer. He cannot feel that his comforts are casually assumed. As I totter over slick and rough patches, helped by a brief flashing of dim light, I would think instead of the rock beneath my feet proverbially containing my primitive ancestors, perhaps some struggling Pleistocene microbe, I want to think instead of those "invisible" workers who, with tools such as wires, wire cutters, pliers, wrists and hands make it possible for one so stupid to reach out her arm and flip on the light switch—whereby seeing without even thinking about it. No, I will not even glance at or notice light waves and particles fleeing down to the gloom of my eye's vitreous to trigger signals among molecular discs with instructions for nerve cables—there to reassemble a picture of what I am seeing (out here on the road) in the back of my mind.

Do I comprehend in even one moment of my making and remaking and ultimate depletion of Energy and Time, just what effort, foresight, and design goes into this making . . . before I am ready to shuffle it all off, or be shuffled out of this recycled body and life? No. I do not comprehend.

Who does then?

Somebody.

It doesn't just happen . . . not any more than it would for an old soul to totter safely in darkness over slick and rough patches, alerting and avoiding intermittent traffic with the flashing of a very weak light.

Somebody had to think this all up; then fashion it all as story. Ongoing episodic story out of that One's own real and creative history, as song, and as life. How does it happened? How does this Somebody do it?

Don't let's think it all guess-work.

Do let's think it is faith

Okay then, a monstrous faith. Because, if not monstrous, if not replete with unfathomable wit and control, then what?

Then nothing?

Nothing at all? (And believe me, I cannot imagine "nothing." Can you?)

And I can only imagine getting safely home in Time to write this, and I cannot imagine the inconvenience and pain, to myself or some innocent driver, of getting hit by a car.

I'll leave that to Another to think of.

Reading *The Hour of Blue* by Robert Froese put out when I was writing the first part of this book 20 years ago, and well worth the reading today. Reminds me just a bit of Edward Abbey—only better. Better in quality and in spirit. Set in Maine, not the desert.

Tuesday, December 29, 2009

Last night was all snow—descending, multitudinous feathery crystals. The a.m. is my gaze upon a slow electric-blue flame pulling long and gently out of red coals behind glass in the soapstone woodstove.

I've written somewhere, maybe in these pages, that free will is the trickiest thing God ever fashioned. Trickier than space-time, multiverse (?), subatomic particles, physical principles and powers (such as gravity and magnetism, molecular motivation, temperature-related expansion and contraction, observer principle); and the extravagant, copious outpouring of everything with its management and minders. Because free will is the manner in which God sets himself apart—even from himself, from all, to observe, as we cannot, what it all means. Like the author trying to get himself out of the story so that its characters might go about their business of living it—miraculously. God is constantly mindful of everything, in profound and exquisite detail—from what goes on in other dimensions at this "moment" to the contents of your own personal stomach in molecules and atoms—nutrients and bacteria, etc. *ad infinitum*. The multitudinous trillions-fold emotional life. Your very thoughts are known at this exact juncture of moments in the plentiful extravagant rational/irrational, loving mind of The Great and Holy God.

Great and Holy God, you say, knowing and momently making and remaking all?—Then why is there base, cruel and malicious torture of the innocents, and the innocence, of God?

Because of free will.

Without free will, limited by laws of what *Is*, limited by laws of creation, nature, and making—without free will there would be no story. Even accidents in which we are injured—those acts wherein laws are disobeyed, not willfully but carelessly, incompetently—are incorporated in the great unfathomable orchestration of everything. C.S. Lewis describes it this way in *The Discarded Image*, (paraphrased): Our past-present-future: In His infinite *Now*, God sees, God does not *foresee*. God's *seeing* does not impinge on our actions.

Many don't believe this, some do, and interesting conversations may ensue. Maybe I'm wrong. The truth is—I'm always wrong, every situation—one cannot help but be wrong, always. Evidence shows I won't get *a nonfiction narrative* right, telling it at secondhand not verbatim. We cannot possibly pour in all the microscopic details of happenings. The only reality is what Is. One knows but little, very little—and, the next moment, what I do know may be wrong. My thoughts about free will are broad, and therefore bound to be wrong. I cannot, for instance, understand how God makes all to *Be* as God goes along doing and thinking, watching and sharing. That is why free will is the trickiest thing God has ever done. does it at this moment while supporting me driving this pen and ink along the page. While believing one might somehow one day be a witness to the contested Big Bang, I do not think I will ever "see"—witness—how free will is actually created. I can only act out my small portion of it, in a limited way.

I learn of limits, some sooner, some later, because of something else God creates, designed and created—*safety*. Living with laws in mind means safety. Cover your mouth when coughing. Slow down when a workman shows you the caution flag. As far as I know, free will is, or would be, the sole justification for retribution. Another name for free will is freedom. We can disobey the sign.

Knock, knock, knocking on Earth's door.

What is my other evidence for free will—besides the torture of innocence before the face of The Holy God? Modesty. God's modesty, retirement of his person, and God's reticence, in "staying off." God's near complete lack of interference since the establishment of all things. God's "need" (wish) to be invited. God will not crash our party, throw God's weight around. Again aside from the necessary violence of creation-in-making. But that too is, perhaps, full of both the personal and impersonal. The "still small voice" is evidence. The gentle invite, silent *word* of caution, impress of desire or delight: to the open, to the willing. To those who ask. Ask. Ask, and it shall be given you. Invite.

Ask to be able to write a tribute to Allen.

Allen, who points out evidence of free will: *the prayer of the Lord Jesus Christ in the Garden of Gethsemane. "Not my will but thine be done."*

Years before we met, I confessed to God: I'm not wise enough to get married, to know *who*. You know, please choose. And then I forgot about it . . . Until after we'd been married awhile.

We sat on the daybed with coffee before the fire, softly talking of what went on yesterday; preparing to ready the coming day out of a dark night's snowfall, night's cunning rest and refreshment of being.

While I was out walking in the slippery dark, yesterday, or sitting on this daybed writing about it, or perhaps I was clearing my desk or eating lunch—don't know what I was doing just at that moment—my spouse was in the paper mill working, minding his own thermographic business. But in the bleachery a valve was stuck open, bleached stock vomiting explosively out of the massive tank cooker, a flood of hot paper stock pushing a worker against the wall. The whole mixer load, bigger than a shipload (with gigantic ship's screw for a beater) blew out into the basement, the bleachery basement, and out into the yard . . . from the basement to a depth—in some places—of three or four feet (it was rumored). The man in charge of the bleachery sustained burns as he stood in deep stock trying desperately to close off a valve, stanch the flow of bleaching, cooking, paper stock made of water, chemicals and the munched up fiber of forests.

It's what happens sometimes in decrepit old mills owned by investors who have no idea what it takes to keep hardware and reinforced concrete viable, pressurized steam under control. So un-carefully is it sometimes done: one switch, a switch, according to thermographic imaging, not in the best of shape, now stands between the mill's power supply, the incalculable public grid, and its ultimate stoppage and freeze-up. Will investors try to imagine what a massive paper mill, bound in girders and concrete, engines and motors, full of chemicals and heats under tremendous pressure, dryers and bleachery and grinders, fast-moving windings, forklifts, iron, and steel: no light and no movement *what ever*? Can *you* imagine it while reading about it on a piece of paper? Naturally investors are not thinking of this but of how one person can be made to do the job of three in order that investors, when casting their eyes over figures, percentages, will feel the warmth of favor and light just touching upon their calculating hearts. Not as warm as the burning sensation of pulp stock while "you" are desperately trying to close a stuck valve.

But there are always laws of redounding, of cause-and-effect, of attraction and repulsion . . . even for investors demanding 13% return on investment. In this instance the repercussions of cleanup, extra overtime hours, heavy equipment repair, dirty stock disposal, refurbishing of expensive motors and other equipment, medical bills, suffering and pain, when "things like this happen." Let's see, where do we put this discarded stock that was bound to make many tons of magazines? Oh, right—out there on the mountain, the sludge dump in its surrounding forest with that scarcely contained runoff and rumored deer-that-aren't-quite-right. Just get it out of the yard before it hardens into a frozen mountain of its own.

What don't I like to read? What don't I enjoy? What do I dislike as humor? Sarcasm. Irony. The dry ironic gaze in literature. Dismayed by examples of what I've just written above. In such use—the sinking sick feeling, that's where the otherwise worthy paper and ink hit the wall in disgust or frustration. The subtle eye, knowing straight face, cold stare as a howl goes up and the wilderness rips up its own ground, snarling.

There is no genuine tribute to the man sitting beside me, coffee in hand, gazing at flames behind glass in the woodstove.

Allen, who returns from work, with steel-toe boots caked in pulp stock, is what is known hereabouts as "getting done," in the paper mill. Next week, he is hoping. The New Year.

The economic health of the region is in this old mill's prospering—has been since the mill began as a gleam in the shrewd eye of Hugh Chisholm, a man studied in contemporaneous 19th-century ways of mill-making, papermaking, acquiring property, logging, and power generation with transport via waterways. It was a bad way of making anything, then as now. Please, I do mean *simply*—but that it might all have been done *carefully and well*. Taking into account *everything* of and in its making. It may be that this was how Strathglass Park was then built, in beautiful period Victorian and Edwardian architecture, as company residences. It *could* be done, now as then.

Allen brought his family here in the late 20th century and, after supporting us in other rural industries (skiing for one) and other types of mills—raw materials were trees—he was taken on by a contractor, prelude to working in the massive paper mill. Our days of stopgap handouts were over. That is, they've been over. No one knows what the future will bring save The Great One watching/writing our story. Experience shows that handouts may be, conceivably, a future way of our care. Experience shows that good health, the ultimate handout, may go the way of everything: Away.

But this decent generous loving kind man has worked in the paper mill for 20 plus years. He provisioned his family. He provisioned me—out of his body and being, his intellectual and emotional life. Out of his sense of duty and purpose, his interior worship and inner life: intuition, communion, conscience. There is where he has known God the Person. There is where he found guidance, spiritual provision, and spiritual correction.

May he now be rewarded in "getting done." May he have physical provision, soulical engagement, and love for evermore. May God never get done making him.

But that would be as God so wills, would it not?

So be it. May we be always ready to pay tribute to the mighty and loving source of all things.

Last Day of the Year at 13%

I woke up at five a.m. to ready for Allen's return from the mill, where he'd been "froze"—a workload of 17 hours in the 24-hour day beginning yesterday morning. This day was to be his last before layoff.

I knew he'd be needing to offload as much of the nightmare as possible before trying to get some rest, a verbal offload onto his loving partner, me. I wanted to record it but did not want to make him self-conscious, so I did it virtually on the sly. Most times it was in my hand not far from his mouth, for my arm rested on the back of the couch, holding the digital recorder. I've recorded such episodes before using cassette recorder, and knew he was comfortable with the idea. Otherwise I would not have done so. And now I was going high-tech.

And here is my transcript of the conversation:

"They wanted to restart the bleachery and they probably would but they won't let them start it without having the scrubber building running. The scrubbery is full of motors and controls for cleaning the pollutants out of gases and fluids used in the process of papermaking. [Coughing, throat-clearing]

"In the scrubber building are a bunch of motors, pretty good-sized motors, this big in diameter [hands and arms stretched, showing 3 ft.], and 5 ft. long. Full of motors, lighting panels, and all the controls. The processor racks are in the same building. Well, when the tank let go, I mean when the tank valve let go [voice weary]—this was a valve that anybody could have operated and let all that—I heard it was 500 tn. of stock. Why they ever put a valve like that—electrically activated—in a place where somebody could do that . . . anyway . . . So the scrubber building took the biggest brunt of it. Filled it up—to a height of 12 ft. inside—every motor and every valve, every processor rack, every lighting panel that was in that building was under water (effectively). [The bleachery tank was 110 ft. tall.]

"When we started doing this last night we had to unhook a lighting transformer that's 12 ft. off the ground. And detach it, completely detach it from the electric system, so the millwrights could remove it and then put another one in. Then we were to get the lights going. And there's no power there so we had auxiliary power from outside come in, and we took circuits apart and hooked—and I did all the wiring—trying to get these lights to go. Every time we plugged a set of lights in, overhead lights, they were—you know these GFCI breakers that we have in the house here?—well everything is protected on the power panel because you got cords running all over the place with water on the floor . . . so they'll have to be protected. So every single one that I plugged into it tripped it. Even the lights got soaked. We think it's just from the moisture that's in the room. They had four large gas heaters going, running full-time while we were working on it. We had to take a processor rack apart and try to dry it. We took all the control modules out of it. I was taking big giant handfuls of bleached stock—gunk—of pulp—out of this cabinet. Big handfuls of it.

"Something was really fun and interesting—'Watch this,' someone said, 'because you're never going to see this again'—We had big lighting panels, about four or 5 ft. long, full of pulp, so we took the fire hose . . . We washed it down with the fire hose . . . [laughing].

"And everybody was working in there—everybody's in everybody else's way. The mechanics are trying to change the motors, line them up with the lasers, electricians are trying to wire them. We're trying to do the lighting panels, and there was like 15 people in the scrubber building (about the size of this house [log cabin]) [sniff, sniffing], trying to work around each other—poor lighting, big gas burners blowing blue flame, water all over the floor, pulp everywhere. It's just like—they'll be lucky if they get anywhere . . .

[He'd been working 17 out of the last 24 hours.] "I got froze so now I got my freeze done. I don't like—don't want to get froze again because I'm laid off and first of all I can't get froze again because they have to go up through the whole list of everybody for freezes mill-wide. And second-of-all, today is my last day. Technically I'm supposed to be working today, but they don't really consider that because they consider that I worked up until six o'clock yesterday [meaning today?]. I got enough hours in with the overtime, that I make, to get 41 hours plus I'm going to get eight hours of straight-time for the holiday. I just can't get into this thing of making a lot of money, and hanging around and going down to the battery shop and trying to sleep there [voice becomes tense]—and somebody eventually catching up with me, and going 'oh, by the way, would you help them out down there in the scrubbery again.' That's all. It was a horror show. The guy that opened that valve was lucky he's alive.

"The offices, where I used to have my office, in central maintenance, had pulp on the floor and the temperature rose—I don't know how they knew this because they would have had to take a [indecipherible] thermometer to know this, but they said—180° in the offices. Because all that pulp came in on the floor . . . They

don't know the whole story just yet. It appears that the guy was trying to open a valve for a bypass to run a pump because they were
repairing a pump, an auxiliary pump . . . Apparently he opened
the wrong valve.

"It was a manual valve originally, but the head of the Kraft
mill, after he had a hard time opening it one time, told them to
install an automatic valve, electrically operated. That could have
been a breach of . . . something . . . safety code . . . Ah, anyway, I
made it through the night."

His night had been a nightmare, the nightmare scenario experienced by
laborers who are expected to work in that hellish atmosphere. One gift that
had been given to them was that of laughter, conversation such as that en-
sued about W. D., the 67-year-old millwright who'd been froze two nights
in a row and now they were trying to page him to come into work again.
Apparently he's got to work until he's at least 71 in order to keep up the
coverage for his wife's medical. He has a great gray beard and is stocky, but
apparently his wife is even bigger and maybe diabetic (if younger), which
is why she can't get Medicare. And one of the anecdotes about W. D. was
concerning the time he was out splitting wood and somehow the wedge
flew up, bashing his lower jaw into his top lip, and blood was pouring everywhere. He came into the house and said matter-of-factly, "You got to
take me to the hospital," but W.D.'s wife, working in the kitchen, said, "Fuck
you, I'm baking bread now." Here's the laughter of people who are living
at an extended pitch—in which people in hell must not infrequently be
called upon to live. Factories, mills, mines, refuse dumps, strip mines and
mountaintop removal.

It was dark in there, light there was hellish, by turns glaring and shadowy, full of the blue and pale rose, the glare of vapor pervading. Sweat,
condensation, dripping off everything, off the workers themselves.

I'd been in the paper mill to watch the process of papermaking first-
hand as part of a tour group. The guides never show rough workings to
tourists. But just standing outside, looking down upon that vast campus,
from your vantage point above, outside of town, you would note right
away, the likeness to your imaginative hell. And yet—it is said—without
this place, there would be no town. Think on that a minute. Would there

still be Indians, Abenaki natives, here? River valley farms? Woodland in old growth trees? We do not know, that would be alternate history.

It wasn't too hard to use this fierce place as a template for hell in speculative fiction. It occurred to me once that it might do very well for a reenactment of Dante's *paradise lost*. (Wink) Naturally, there are all kinds of myths to be mined while working on such themes. One is the mythic dog: the hell hound. He was too good *not* to use in a story like that. Of course I used him. By an odd coincidence, the investment Company which bought the paper mill where Allen works, with the expectation of a 13% return on investment—its emblem is the three headed dog, Cerberus.

All of this hellish three-headed doggedness, to make paper for magazines and books (which so enrich life) . . . but—and this is where I expect the hellishness comes from—to squeeze out an investment of 13% without having to pay. What is left unpaid is contingency labor, the worthy earth and water and air, the sun and the moon and the stars and even the look in a baby's eye. None of these things are taken into account as the cost of doing business. But they are part of the cost, and always will be. And I suspect that digitizing all our words and hitting send will not put a stop to the sluggish and devilish wastefulness and junk.—Doesn't it cost the Earth a lot more in raw material, energy consumption, labor and just plain making for electronic reading devices?

Contrived, planned, obsolescence. Well, after all that, Allen says they still did not get much accomplished there. And of course it's ongoing this day, now the second day of the year as I write. This is what happens when you need 13% instead of enough *people* to make the paper, keep the mill running safely, have enough rest to make the right choice to open the right valve—when one worker is doing the work of three.

Or is this what it costs to have a three-headed dog for an investment counselor?

In that case, isn't it a hopeful thing to "get done?"

Author's note: ten years from now the owners will be Nine Dragons, (Chinese owned.)

January

January 6, 2010

Maine in Winter was not begun as a metaphor of aging but dips down into that theme, owing to current reality. I was 20 years younger on beginning the book. Despite what the Preacher says (that all is vanity), old age is not vanity because it is reality. Reality is not for humanity's imagining, nor that of its individuals. No one but God knows the contents of the next moment. Reality *is the imagination* of God. We are sometimes in tune with it, sometimes not. Yet, paradoxically, coming and going through our minds, *vain imagining* is *actual*—meaning what is *not* real is part of what *is* real in that moment. It is when I *act* on my unreal imagining that my freedom meets its constraint.

I went snowshoeing and then wrote about it, commenting on and evaluating, the "intrusion" of old age in the pursuit. Old-person-snowshoeing is reality? I do need, for desire and well-being, to be active—be outside feeling the snowing, the freshness, coming fierceness and swaying of stiff limbs (trees' stiff limbs, not my own). I came back with irritated toes in the cycle of rubbing-induced pain—small injury—which may prohibit snowshoeing until a tiny wound is healed. But the great and good thing is *lightly* to bear it.

Some people have a heavier reality to bear than others. Superman for one, Christopher Reeves. He had a heavy reality to bear after an equine fall, following his elegant life as a star. He allowed himself, as quadriplegic, a full hour of self-pity each day before getting down to the business of his new reality. A lot of his new work involved helping people in like condition. I might say he was broken on the laws of physics and afterwards salvaged his life with submission to reality. Note the root relationship of this word with that of the word *saved*. He was salvage after the accident and bore it well.

So well was it done that, I would guess, he engaged personally with God. (Perhaps during that hour of self-pity.)

Today we went out on snowshoes again, intending to break trail past downed hemlocks in woods beyond our neighbors. One does not notice the weight and tug of snowshoes upon the toes until there's a sore. A bit of raw slightly infected flesh no bigger than a square millimeter—rubbing—prevented my continuing on the shoes. Prevented me: from lifting the snowshoe, heavy itself, heavy with clinging snow—rubbing against the top of but one small toe. Allen decided to stay behind as well. He climbed up back of the house to keep that bit of trail open, but I had to return inside, disappointed. If only I were Superman. Superman—over a tiny bit of raw flesh? Yes. I'd like that.

Allen says the Midwest is getting hit hard this winter, with snow and cold; and that we seem to be missing it. But 22°F this Thursday on waking, this January 7, 2010. I stood on our deck and was refreshed in dim silence by movement around my legs—the faintest winter breeze. It seemed my lower extremities were in rags. Pajamas and robe, under the overcoat. I listened quietly to its further extent—somewhere back up there on the mountain ridge behind me. Faint, soft, intimate.

Later, as light lifts, Allen gives *me* a lift to the end of the frozen pond . . . to test the foot-doctoring and get much-needed exercise. A somber hill flanks the north pond off my left shoulder across the expanse. Ahead an icy road rises and disappears, downwards, away. I verge instead into a lane edging the pond studded with colorful camps. Or, as known elsewhere, "cottages."

Crane my neck to see past tall pines in said colorful camps, wanting to know if ice fishing ensues. Don't think it can. Hasn't been cold enough, long enough. I come out of this lane into the open, seeing a shoreline cut with snowmobile track near its bank. A break in ice and there's water. The pond's expanse beyond is pure dim light without track, without trail, without ice fishing shacks, equipment, or fishermen.

Nothing but purity and desolation I love.

Walking down into that narrow dead end vale where we live, up the hill and down past a neighboring house, I smell "things." The cold, I notice, sometimes enhances or particularly conveys scent. Especially cold with stillness. Sudden cigarette smoke with no one around. A smell of laundry detergent, of fabric softener. The heavy surprisingly sweetish scent of un-burnt—partly combusted—household furnace fuel-oil.

Thursday p.m. January 7, 2010

They are talking about the relative merits of ax versus saw, bucksaw or handsaw. Our friend says he was given a gift today: He found a buyer for his chainsaw. For many years now he has been getting in firewood with the chainsaw, cutting wood off his property. This sale means, as he says, more time spent in woods, more exercise, making efficient use of one's strength.. That—he and I agree—is fine. *More time spent in the woods.* The chainsaw has its merits but these are outweighed by more-time-spent-in-woods. When needing firewood to survive in winter someone possessed of health and love of work will rejoice that every day there's an activity requiring one to spend more time etc. . . .

Demerits include kickback and possibly grave injury with the chainsaw, pollution and use of two-stroke gas. Noise. If you use one all day as loggers do, you need hearing protection as well as chaps and other gear protective against kickback. Statistically, logging and mining are the most dangerous jobs in the U.S.. But with regard to axe versus saw, as discussed by Allen and friend: An axe, with strength, will bring down a tree with danger too.

Chips galore, small, but can be gathered for home fuel. The handsaw can be used to cut a wedge from a trunk before felling. A wedge goes into the woodstove along with sawn and split stove-wood. A mall with sledge-hammer splits wood. A bucksaw is a fine tree-taking saw. He plans to take down his small trees, leave the big ones to keep adding girth, and use such clearings for corn. These would probably need only lime that first year (or lots of wood ash). Nutrients abide in woodland topsoil but Maine forest duff is shallow. Underneath it is sand, mineral, silt and clay. When Maine topsoil is used for crops, add ashes or lime. Plant legumes to pull nitrogen from air.

A bucksaw, used with sawbuck, can cut up to 6 ft. lengths. But our friend says he'll try a machete type knife he is making to lop down thick saplings.

Story Three-Ways

On a cold winter's day when you almost can't move, it's nice to sit by the fire reading.

The explorer's dream of *Norumbega* (as Maine was once known) is part of Maine's history; a mistake from maps of exploration composed by cartographers in Nuremberg, Germany. But Norumbega became the fabled land of gold somewhere up the Penobscot River in Maine. Fabled land *that never was* . . . but somehow still exists in a mythic and historic imagination.

The narrator of *The Hour of Blue* muses on place names while in Manhattan for a job interview. Sometimes I want to live long with a book, reenter its pages after weeks or months to continue this story at whose end I have not yet arrived. Willie Collins' *No Name* lay on the floor behind our couch six months before I picked it up to finish. Floors can be dust-mopped while a book moves about. I keep myself in touch with these "other" individual worlds, sometimes for years. *The Hour of Blue* is like that. And now, after several months, I have just begun reading its epilogue. But lengthy reads should not be so unusual: it takes me far longer to *write* a book—while inhabiting that world. Imaginatively inhabit its characters over a period of time. I do not say I'm getting to know the author, per se, when I read something. But what *interests* the author. As reader I am really getting to know, in common with the writer, his or her *muse* . . . Maybe the craft, the sensibility, whatever, is private, captured there on the page and shared with a reader's imagination—so I guess even there, this is a collaboration, three ways.

A three-way collaboration: muse-writer-reader. *The Hour of Blue* is a stitching together, an interleaving of history, faux history, science, faux science, myth, and Maine's natural world, its environmentalism. The ragtag industrial coastal setting with diners and taverns and banks and houses, camping, motels . . . Its pacing is quiet and lifelike and rural; its narrator's sensibility lifelike and quiet, almost a matter-of-fact telling in minutia. Lots of what daily life is really like here, interspersed with the telling of Maine's flaws, with its pain (quietly done). Yet it is a work of speculative fiction, the fantastic, telling a truly outlandish idea with outlandish and spiritual repercussions.

This work of Robert Froese's reminds me of Edward Abbey's (a bit), again, without the desert, and maybe John Nichols' (The Voice of the Butterfly) without its energy and profanity. Should I mention there is a chapter section titled "The Frankenstein Effect"?

About our walk on the snowroad in tandem with the little Androscoggin River. . . . But I stop to lament my lack of desire for this work, these books of

Maine memoir or creative essays. Even after writing three or four of them I regret that there is no interest on the part of anyone for these books. That I'm not interested myself makes it harder. And my *fiction* holds little interest beyond my own. That interest makes the doing worthwhile. They can be done to questionable perfection because they are fantastic, based upon any story-land. I have loved throughout my life what the world calls unreal. But I do wonder if story-land is more true and actual than what we call *real*. What's in the text *does not change*. Memory changes our experience. That is, memory is faulty, distorts.

Reality disappears every moment into memory, a kind of story-land . . . but one whose reach is long because of morality—the cause and effect, "sowing and reaping," of actions from the past. God's "memory" is not faulty. And earlier, but coinciding somewhat with this, I've wondered if morality is the sole indestructible quality. Maybe "quality" is not the right word. What is morality?

Morality is living, alive, some kind of Being, God . . . But not in the sense in which I think God is Time, or God is Energy, or God is Space, the Universe without clothes. God, I think, is all these solely because they are so great that God is the Only One capable of assuming them as His garments. Even as apparel these cannot contain God. He Alone is responsible but also delegates, gives instruction, and receives accountability, stewardship for various aspects of Creation. But morality is different. I do not think it is made, or created.

Morality is what God is. Just as God is Love. And I think God has "always been" Morality. It is maybe the essential Person, himself. All things can be "destroyed" and remade into other things, but not that. Morality cannot be corrupted. It can, for a time, be "ignored" by what is itself corrupt . . . but that ignoring or even ignorance is but *seeming* only temporary. Corruption is contemptuous of goodness. Self is a spirit claiming to be like God, claiming, when the self thinks it can get "away" with it, to be God. But self is corrupt and may wear a subtle appearance of morality, or even an *apparent* morality. One seeing this appearance may or may not fooled, but the moralizer is self-fooled. *(Wink)* Corruption is contempt for God.

All the above musing-in-ink is just me thinking aloud on the page. All positive soundings *should* be followed by question marks here? And what happened to our walk on the snow road?

It's said that if something is boring to write about, its readers will be bored as well. The Sunday walk was at once painful, uncomfortable, tedious, prolonged *and* invigorating, refreshing, pure, inquisitive, companionable, remembering. The square quarter inch of raw and sometimes infected wound on the top of the third toe, left foot, was somewhat in evidence, but vying competitively for attention with other hurting parts of me: both feet, the leg, jaw, neck. Walking into the cold buffeting wind pulls tension on bodily fibers throughout, but seems to localize in my jaw. As though a fist gathering, pulling and twisting taut every ligament, tendon, and muscle fiber connected throughout my frame—right there on either side of my jaw. Tension, from whatever cause, seems to gather there. But the tiny wound was helped because I walk without snowshoes. It's considered a devilish work to pour salt into a wound but in fact it is healing, drawing out the infection. Should we then dispose of the salt-in-wound metaphor?

—You're not enjoying this part of our walk?

The snow road is a wide groomed snowmobile road winding through woodland, avoiding marshes and bogs but not wet shallow places—these freeze when others do not. The stream is sounding and open in places, visible on the left-hand, the Little Andy, through dark trunks etched with grey-green lichen. Big glacial erratics stand stockstill. The white road winds around, continuing deep into woodland territory.

Territory familiar to me in its green or budding garments, and awfully choked with downed limbs left by loggers in other years. So much has been uncovered from those cutting years: near-naked, white slopes off our right shoulders, Allen's and mine, as we walk on; sometimes speaking of events current to us, and small to the rest of the world not similarly occupied: Would Allen make it past tomorrow in the mill?

He has been called back, but this time on the construction crew. Allen is almost 64 and not in the best shape to be doing heavy electrical industrial construction work. He has, apparently, lost the job he was good at, infrared technician, having trained a younger more able-bodied man in the technique and equipment—one who, by his build, would be better suited to construction work. But we shall see, what will be.

This was the logging road that did me injury a few years back when it was wearing green. The year or two after my partial hip replacement, if I remember right. I recollect the time because it happened after Allen bought me a "girl's bike" so-called for its skirt-dip frame—easier to dismount. Less likely to catch me up, send me sprawling. On this trail, now buried white here in the valley between big hills, I followed the then uncovered river of tree bones, dragging my new bike, first over runoff ditches meant to halt road erosion, perhaps three miles lugging my bike there, and then through a river of limbs. Hard work and exhausting for one then not quite 60 who likes to heap mental-and-ink-labor as well. Add that day's labor to a Sunday's labor which should have been left undone for faith's sake, and it added up to break-down for me. As nerve endings came unsheathed—nervous breakdown.

Well.

I was writing fiction about two or three whiners, one or two of which complained almost constantly about *being*. Much like the maker of Frankenstein's monster, Victor Frankenstein himself. But also *the monster*. Nothing like real life to give one a feel for storybook characters . . . yes?

However, in this instance, story-land bestowed on me an understanding of my real life. I had already written all that fiction about the impossibility of being responsible for *being* when—what should happen?—I experienced the possibility/ impossibility myself. I haven't counted out the instances in which collaboration with God kindles epiphany. But it does give one pause while in the act of sub-creating. Especially when scary things happen to one's characters . . . or one's characters take on scary adventurers or responsibilities. Sub-creating takes on the surprising profound weight of collaborative insight. I notice, as well, that creative people aren't always well-made. Moral fiber often missing. Can be awful whiners. Complainers, tedious. Looking for the easy escape. Conversely, often hard workers. Driven.

The trail was packed and corrugated by snow machines, crisscrossed with footprints of critters, birds, varying hares, mice, deer. The occasional very short human trail off to one side signifying people's universal need to off streams of mortal refuse. (Note the subtle euphemism.)

When we turn back, tired but refreshed by the snow road, we look forward to good things to eat and drink. There may also be a couple of massages . . . and kind companionship. One of the many compensations of a long, collaborating marriage.

Tuesday, January 12, 2010

Took Allen to work at the paper mill, struck anew by its smell as we drove into a lot at the lower gate—a penetrating chemical-vegetable stench on heavily laden mists, steams, smokes billowing up and down, and roiling over the river, the lot, the chip piles. Gray monolithic structures where trees are re-created into coated paper. "Paper is made in hell"—the name of a short narrative nonfiction piece inspired by this place—itself burned and sifted ashy on the snowy wind outside my bedroom window. My job today is application for Social Security, in preparation for us to live when work in the paper mill is over for Allen. What I prayed for in the first part of these books. Allen was getting started there then.

So I drop him off in better shape than when he went in yesterday expecting to be on the construction crew. He is back on the thermographic work and looks to be doing three big surveys between now and his hoped-for self-imposed retirement date around the end of March—early retirement. About one year before age 65, the previously sanctioned retirement date.

I drive out of the lot leaving my woolen gloves behind on the ground in a turnaround—ignorant of the fact . . . this sudden minor detail of God's great creating in this minor subsection of Space & Time.

Space and Time. Just from curiosity: What was I doing 12 years ago? Twelve years ago there was no me, whether of Time, Space or Materials, for my very molecular makeup has changed so that what was is no more. Not only do we never step into that same river twice, we are not the same person twice to step into the river. My body deteriorates into its next form as I speak, and the other parts of my being—emotion, intellect, will; memory, personality, perception: all different, not the same. Not even very like . . . while yet being recognizably me or even, temporarily, my own. Decrepitude of body and bodily influence does not mean the same for being's other elements. What of my moral being? Does it disintegrate? It seems to me it does, but maybe I am just learning myself, my soul, better.

It is obvious to me in looking at this inky messy page that my spelling disintegrates, my handwriting does, my wrist action. But what use I am to the muse—at this moment—increases. The craft has increased with practice. Years upon years of practice. Once, and not long ago in space and time, this page was blank except for evenly spaced gray lines on a plain background of cream.

I drove out of Rumford without my gloves. Of course, like Chekhov's gun, they will be mentioned again, even used again one day. All details and placement of same are known to the Creator and will be used of the Creator in Time. No matter how seemingly frivolous or inconsequential. That's the thing about the gun. Sometimes it's not used as a shotgun but as a conversation piece. And sometimes it's not even a shotgun . . . but a pistol . . . or a muzzleloader . . . or a woolen glove. Two woolen gloves.

Let's see. Before I got diverted into that crafty subject I was going to check my journal of some years back to see what I was doing on this date minus those years . . . I have nothing written on January 12. But, January 11, 1998?—close enough.

First some notations written by Allen, beginning in Florida, January 1998, ending in our Maine rental:

> *79° in morning at sunrise. Storms eastern seaboard and NE [New England]. Storms across Florida. Ice, freezing rain in Maine. Son calls and tells us the power is out. I call Pan Am and change our return flight to the ninth. So we can keep our apartment from freezing up.*
>
> *Jan. 9, 1998. We go to airport. Find our flight is delayed 3 1/2 hours. Decide to change back to the chance. JD calls, says Maine is in the state of emergency. I shoot a photo of a dove on an electric pole. Take some shots by the Caloosahatchee River.*
>
> *Jan. 10, 1998. Getting ready to return. Early in sunshine. Route 26 closed. Ice. Stayed overnight at Motel 8.*
>
> *Jan. 14, 1998. Maine declared a disaster area 15 out of 16 counties. Power still out here. Keeping warm with woodstove, water from spring. Plenty of photo ops with ice on limbs.*
>
> *Jan. 15. No power yet. 2° overnight, what a contrast to Fort Myers last week. 82,000 CMP customers still out. Public radio dependable [with batteries].*
>
> *Jan. 23. Power has been back on for one week. Another messy storm approaching. -4° overnight. Going to meet with JD for lunch. Florida and ice storm slides are back.*

Sunday, January 11, 1998

Home from Fort Myers into the aftermath of ice storm '98; 500,000 people (185,000 CMP and Bangor Hydro "household customers") without power since four days ago. The longest largest outage ever here in Maine. Trees are bowed with ice, every branch and twig. Driving through reminded me of mountains' scape and rime. O'Rouke's woodstove proves the Lord's care of us. We are warm now here. Lise stayed upstairs to watch over the place until we returned. She's gone in search of shower and friends and warmth—an excellent neighbor. We are at the end of a rural road and will be one of the last to have power. Estimates range 4–10 days.

3 million people in Quebec without power seven days.

1-17-98. Power on (for us) yesterday. Thousands are still without.

That was the year and place—time and space—I dealt myself (for God's own purposes) irrevocable damage. Or damage irrevocable to my plantar fascia, right foot. Chronic damage from kicking at three inches of ice. Water frozen to the density of marble. Rock is, of course, frozen magma, or frozen metamorphosed sedentary rock (compacted and tempered to strength). Surrendered to a certain temperature, granite will unfreeze and become molten. Water takes less time and elemental cooling to acquire similar density, concreteness of rock and ice compared to flesh and tendons. My excellent neighbor offered me a ride across the ice in her pickup. Don't know why I declined. Pride perhaps. Deliver me!

How did I damage my foot seemingly for all time? All the time allotted to me?

I merely wanted to walk on slick ice 3 to 5 in. thick without falling. If I could make it across the yard to the cleared and sanded road I'd be good to walk 3 mi. round-trip to the store. To the post office. Anywhere away from the cabin fever I was coming down with after that ice storm.

Medical knowledge acquired in the account: If one repeatedly breaks ice with one's heel, even stiffly booted, the plantar fascia will become inflamed. If one then walks three miles on emerging inflammation . . . Chronic injury results. Pain for the rest of your time. Treatments, expense, casts, orthotics, exercises, painkillers, therapy with golf balls, massage, love increasing in a watchful spouse. Deep regret. Rocky woodland walks with my pal pain. I rejected a ride across the concrete ice that would have prevented this injury.

Fear not, gentle reader. Suffering will serve its purpose. We are loved.

12 years later I go to the Social Security office in Rumford on the other side of the canal from its paper mill. I have lost, and God has recovered, many things over the course of my life. I've lost winter at least 62 times, and 63 times it has returned. I've lost baubles, rings, coins, tokens, friends . . . and God has helped me recover them. Yes, I have asked God personally to help me find things lost. God likes being asked—not for thrones, dominions—but for small things.

Take that pair of gloves left behind in the lot at the lower gate to hell. I spent time today looking for those patched woolen gloves. Checked all my coats' pockets, shelves where we keep such things. Out-of-the-way places, searched my mind, got an inkling they'd fallen out of my lap—when I got out of the car at the mill to take over driving as Allen went into work.

On pulling down past a line of parked cars in the evening I spotted one glove near that spot I had vacated earlier in the day. It took another 10–15 minutes of asking and looking. That second glove was found in a very narrow space between two vehicles, a car and pickup bearing the vanity plate TINY.

Thank you, most high God for bothering to show me where the wind had hidden that woolen glove. It was a fierce wind, howling through Rumford and tightening my jaw as I walked its narrow painful mountain canyons. Those brick blocks hemmed in by God's plutonic mountains feel like canyons when the wind is cold and fierce, streets icy, and I'm walking into it hugging my Dunkin' coffee. You are not a genie in a bottle to come at my beck and call, supplying my wishes, three wishes to make me rich and famous . . . or even kind . . . against your will.

But you helped me find my woolen gloves.

Thursday, January 14, 2010

The Way We Live Now by Anthony Trollope is very funny. Almost the only places I laugh aloud, while listening to the 100 chapters of this hefty tale, is when he writes of authoress Lady Carbury's surface abject humiliation in trying to get reviews of her work. In this book he shows how well he knows us. Us writers, us humans. The chapters 1 and 89 are the best for his takes on the question of book reviews in the 19th century. The whole book is amazing in its likeness of our own times, especially in portraying the fantastic world of finance; politics, tabloid journalism (i.e. all journalism), the double-ness playing in almost any transaction, and the honorableness that might avail instead. He's dead on in so many aspects of us as we are now but what has changed is women as chattel, as bargaining chip, token to be put to use here or there. This kind of control or use is now in her hands—in current western secular society. . . . Plus, the narrator does crack me up when he goes on about "American women."

Dealing with cabin fever this week. Out walking the star-choked a.m. from Johnny's Bridge. This road along North Pond is clear—no need for ice-walkers here. Forgot my reflectors but have small flashlights in either hand. Eight degrees and very still. I don't tense up as when the wind blows. My head does not throb. The immensity spans above me as I walk sometimes singing made up songs to God explaining everything and regretting my trivial mind . . . This star-stitched immensity is a big bright and profound encouragement. Unworthy thoughts—do you ever lament the triviality or spite of your thoughts? I do every day. Deeply admire the theoretical physicist his or her thought-life. Deeply grateful to be a fiction writer so that for at least some long moments I might be relieved of my baseness, silliness, improper fancy and lowdown pettiness. Hooray for the overwhelming vigor and universal enormity of Creation!! Hooray for breath! The slow gas exchange with trees, glory of stars snared in their branches, or streaking swiftly through deep atmosphere. Pale as a comet but instant, quick, neither steady nor prolonged . . .

Later, on the walk back, faint light limning Spruce Mountain, I listen, again, to *The Way We Live Now.* Would I want my fiction reviewed? I do. Would anyone be interested in publishing creative nonfiction to come out of my pen? They would not. . . . Unless the fiction goes anywhere? Then Yes. Is that likely to happen? I think so. In my "lifetime"? No! Do I pine? Would I publish this? Not if I were a "real" publisher.

—Trivial.

Which brings me back to my heroine, Annie Dillard. She never resorted to self-promotion. She has said so. I've not seen any. And I believe it's true. But—on the other hand—she has not had to. What if there'd been no promotion of her work by others? I believe she'd go with obscurity instead of self-promotion. Likely she would formally, "go through proper channels," submit and receive rejection. Not try networking. She would leave her work unread, unwanted by others and not be able to sell it. Fact remains: She did not need to. It happened. And God did it. Why? Because she would not do it herself? Because God wanted it done? To the last, at least, yes. But me? I do network. A little. I do self-promote. A little.

But I don't activate comments. I wouldn't know what to say.

Friday, January 29, 2010

Sitting in the dark-fire-flickering room of our log cabin with Allen, sipping coffee. He got up first, made coffee and fire. Eight degrees out and wind blowing. We sit not speaking, listening to the wind. High above, northwestward sounding—there; beyond the pinewood ceiling, but high. It stays there marshaling, roaring, but a piece of wind comes down, begins speaking with the log house, parts of the house, the roof, under the roof; the house moaning back. I hear it, feel its draft between the logs; me wrapped up here on the futon, upright. The wind speaks differently in various woodland hauntings—given the contour of these hills, narrowness of the vale not far below. Fir-heavy conifers, pines with long needles, naked deciduous branches. I've been praying. *Forgive me, make me kind . . .* The wind breathes at the front door sucking, seething; speaking with the door and frame, tiny gap in its lower right corner. Is it the door speaking, the house? Is it the wind? Or is it a mutual conversation?

Maine's January thaw is over. I haven't written of it though it too is part of winter. It rained, a stream at the foot of our wooded lot rising, carrying dead branches before it, blocking part of a culvert. I'd been working on this book during a thaw, trying to cobble something together. Trying to smooth—make promising, engaging—with that first part of the book. Not easy. Not very lively workings yet, front to back. Lots of fixing, patching, hooking—not so much intentional interweaving.

I'm tired but ongoing. *Gotta be. Gotta do.* Looking forward to rest at the end of each day. I've been reading an online story "Being Real" and . . . I'm all for it so far. One thing I read for—sometimes the only thing, even above craft: Sensibility. It's got to be fair or I'm gone. Could not do Elmore Leonard. His prime value, I've read, is *cool*. The Cool, *be cool*. Flippancy in evil won't do for me. Same city, different sensibility, and of course with its being YA . . . But not that only. At the end, I found "Being Real" confusing, but maybe that's the point?

A banging and *bok*ing. Things thudding, cracking, falling: wooshing, wooing, rattling. The wind speaking with things. Things, even, of its making, placing, displacing.

"I just feel like cataloging the sounds it's making with everything," I said to Allen; leaned back, closing my eyes.

Sat forward, wrote more. It was light now. If I wanted, I could verbalize visual movements the wind was creating.

His breath in my ear, Allen leaning over, blowing on me. Eyes closed, I smiled, laughed. "Wooing," he said. And got up to do some work.

Saturday, January 30, 2010

Praying the Father that I would love Him: God.

Out on the deck in -1° and wind blowing, moonlight so low round and bright—easy to see up into these woods, hatch work of the real and shadow trees. The moon itself looks huge there . . . low in its sky. Allen will mention this as the moon's being 30,000 miles closer in perigee than we usually see. But the *sound* of things out here I notice most. Allen will say that colder air density makes for bigger soundings. The brushing of the push broom, *crack* of the broom-end reporting as I knock off snow crystals laid down yesterday—right where I wanted to stand and pray in my slippers and robe, overcoat. Where the big light sits in a vacuum of space—nothing out there to carry such sounds. I'm told Native Americans have called this the wolf moon, a full moon occurring on the day it's at perigee.

. . . In a wind so sweeping and cold as fire when I step from the house-shelter on the wooden deck with the broom. Then I lean against the rail, itself cracking like a tree about to fall in woods above.

It was 52° inside. The hardwired fire alarm went off at 4 a.m. Allen got up to go down to the cellar and pull a fuse switch—couldn't find the right one at first in the dark. Its piercing reverberated throughout the house, intensifying in my ears as I passed beneath the alarm. A mystery why this happened. No present fire, smoke, exhaust.

The fire in the woodstove is very hot, hotter than usual for the time it's been burning, and with a deep propane-blue flame pulling up from red-orange coals.

"Does this denser air make that happen, too," I asked, "the fire burn hotter?"

"It's got more oxygen in it.—What fire needs to burn."

Tomorrow Allen and friend will go up into these woods to cut cedar. They will use cedar to make sawbucks.

February

Hour of Grey

AND I WAS OUT on our deck in the hour of grey, sometimes called dusk, sometimes the hour of blue. And glancing up among trees so numerous and straight above, tall grey trunks against a lighter shade of snow, against a dim sky. I saw faint movement, scarcely to be seen, the white tail. Yes, a whitetail. And I stopped to watch among those grey boles. And saw the grey deer, its winter coat grey, stepping high among trees. Tentative, cautious. And I stood still. And watched it and its family come through trees along the slope above. A clump of hemlock intervened, small hemlocks, between my gaze and their passing. I watched for them to come out the other side but they did not. And then I knew they had found their lying down places up there above our path.

Sometimes one must look out how to end a book. Sometimes a book ends itself abruptly, emphatic, leaving the author to say, "That's it?" After a few moments the certainty becomes real. I had another *In Winter* book, finished some years ago. Fiction. Had no idea how to end, but I felt its strength giving out and that it must end soon. Two characters are left alone, lovers, talking, drawing near. But one of them . . . Certainly the author felt her groping—troubled—but not defeated. Like what the story's ending itself seemed. I let it go at that. But the cycle itself, of which it was but a part, ended in the first way—emphatic and abrupt . . . When its author had thought it would go on . . . and find a different ending after maybe one more adventurous scene, or two or three.

What's with all our story endings? Some do hardly end but leave every character ongoing into . . . maybe snow fall? Yes, that's it. They go into falling snow, blending into the dim blue picture. Mysterious, unknown to us. Themselves unknowing.

When we reach the first of February I always feel winter somehow failing. But it is cold on waking, maybe in the teens Fahrenheit, or maybe as predicted for tomorrow's a.m. -3°. Even when, as it is said, Maine winter goes on. And on. Until July.

I've wondered how to end this book simply, because I'm tired. Tired of this Winter Book, begun 20 years ago and dropped after several entries over the course of two 21st century winters until this present Winter. I'm tired of *Maine Metaphor*. In fact I have enough material for one more, *The Gulf*, and I plan to do it. But, as said, I've never cared much for these.

They have been a great help to my other writing, imparting much understanding in detail of Maine. Fiction interests me. Fiction has not happened to me. Therefore, like real life, it is primary experience. Writing nonfiction, narrative nonfiction—*Maine Metaphor*—*recording* what is *primary* experience does not interest. Not interested in *recollecting* the primary. Recordkeeping is lifeless to me. Sometimes, maybe even often, it may come to life again . . . But only after or during serious work. Research, re-imaging the subtext, the theme; probing and governing metaphor; seeking, finding insight. Smoothing out, applying prose skills, reworking: Then it may become primary again, this work. It may.

Tomorrow, when it's below zero, I'll be in Lewiston, town of the Androscoggin River Falls . . . May walk the city street going from the lab to the endoscopic unit of the hospital. Or I may take the shuttle. I like to walk, even though it will be windy, bitter cold. Hard underfoot. I love that kind of thing, that kind of walking. It wakes me up, enlivens. Not so those pains afterward.

There are to be blood tests and a biopsy. Won't take more than a second or two, that last part, they say, in and out retrieving the nearly microscopic specimen. And we won't know results until next week. I think this is a good way to end the book. Not knowing the outcome of these tests. I don't need wrap-ups anymore . . . to make engaging the story. When I'm reading.

I love to read.

That's how I got into this writing life.

I see by the 1990 log that 20 years ago today, a Thursday, were routine devotions, the Lord's passion. Then down to the town post office to collect mail. After that I typed another draft of the *MM* migrations entry about being in the dentist chair, the dentist's hands, God working on me.

Briefly I experienced the puckering of my retina, that stained-glass look. And I rested. Made lunch, did chores; snow shoveling and worked more on that entry.

Snowing

Late yesterday afternoon we donned traditional snowshoes. Tubbs webbed snowshoes, first made in Norway, Maine, 1906, by Mr. Walter Tubbs. He supplied polar expeditions for Peary and Byrd. Tubbs and Norway went on to produce large orders for the US government during the two world wars. So many jobs, making this wonderful hide-and-ash webbed shoe here, gone now to Guangzhou, China; thanks to "stewards," of political and corporate lobbyists, not our nation's *people*. We tightened the bindings, gripped our poles and climbed out of the driveway surrounded with snow plow-rows.

Winter this year is a mild one. Conditions for shoeing are the worst I've seen since we began shoeing that winter of my partial hip replacement. After the shattering of bone on granite rock. After the accident, Allen bought the shoes merely to keep me on my feet, active. The *positive surprise* of that accident!

Oh, those white-floored woods full of brokenness beneath fresh austere covering. The years—like last year and the year before—when snow is deep and pure—those years of great shoeing. What's always underneath but covered?—broken bits of leafless plants and fallen limbs, rocks—all, covered in thick rich brightness enough to fill eyes and breath with the intricate crystalline life of its mysterious creation.

We went crunching through the byways of our small patch, tall with conifers and leafless others, and great hulking bug-and-bird ravaged standing trees. And over the stream and into the tree tunnel between the stream and road.

When viewed from the comfort of a warm cabin here in Maine, falling snow is quiet, mysterious and evocative. It may be the result of a Nor'easter slowly turning its mystical counterclockwise whiteness above us, while Gulf of Maine moisture is crystallized in air. Rarely is it caused by a blizzard plunging down out of the north. Maine's temperatures seldom fall rapidly enough to denote *blizzard* which is common in Montana and Wyoming. Yet we can and do get fantastic amounts of the pristine geometrical stuff in the western mountains, northern uplands, and, on occasion, along the steel-blue coasts.

Collected by NOAA, from Maine's 30-odd weather stations, the compilation of data from these reports, over 60 or 70 years, gives us a numerical picture of Maine's varying snowfall—from the wet coast to our frigid mountains, and barren, windswept, Aroostook plains/hills. Maine, according to the Northeast Regional Climate Center, which uses NOAA's data, is New England's whitest state. This takes into account that great, or mini depending on your point of view, snow king Mount Washington, in New Hampshire. In the north where the maximum 30-year means are found (1951–1980), the range is from 123 in. per year at the Ripogenus Dam to an aberrant low of 93 in. in northerly Presque Isle. I call it aberrant because Caribou, just one town north of Presque Isle, records a mean of 120 in.. (All these figures are from the last century, when I was working on snow amounts for an undergraduate course in Maine geography.

But when it's a lean snow year as is this one (so far), shoeing means breaking through crusts and snagging snowshoe webbing on dead twiggy limbs underfoot—under *this* season's snow covering. You don't like sticking to trails because it's interesting to get off through trees and into undesignated territory—and usually snowmobilers have crushed down the trails you might otherwise use. Then the surface may not require massive alien webbed feet. In fact, if one's foot hurts from chronic injury brought on by stubbornness in a former distant year, it feels like shoeing on pavement.

When we get to our neighbor's the track is broken by another neighbor's machine. His has no sled (as snowmobiles are called here), but a four-wheeler (ATV) with track treads installed specially for winter terrain. He loves exploring the mountain trails old settlers' once made and used with horse and oxen; now skidder trails used by loggers to get the wood out. (Above our house are mostly intermittent working industrial forests.) His twin tracks are wide enough that we can go down their middle on snowshoes. Fine, depending on conditions, but we're hankering to get off into puckerbrush. Where no track—not even our own—has gone before.

A week ago: before going up-mountain behind the house on my own, I left Allen a note about my plans (roughly). Because he was down at the coast and would need that info when he got back if I weren't there to greet him. Can anything express the feeling I had climbing up back there through those tangles on my bear claws? These Tubbs shoes are equipped to grip the steep incline. I could not have done it without them.

But, hold on. One might be disappointed to see what my steep grade climb is part of. The true athlete would smile. We live down an old now dead-end surrounded by low wooded mountains, old slopes rounded down to their ancient plutonic hardness. They are not the splendid sharp proud more sedimentary counterparts in the American and Canadian Northwest. There the Giants are mantled in height and youth scarcely crumbled in comparison to our (formerly higher than the Rockies) eroded Appalachian bumps. Our mountains at base are closer to sea level than those giants mid-continent. What can I say of our more humble attitude (and altitude)? Maine's mountains are near sea level. Thus, in the numbers, they lose much in awe.

I scrambled as my feeble and somewhat broken abilities allowed. I grasped what handholds were offered by saplings and larger trunks while still keeping hold of my poles. And often I leaned against a great bole, panting, having obtained footing there by precarious means. I belong to that demographic known as retirees. Older than I was by 20 plus years since beginning this book. This *Maine Metaphor in Winter* was begun on what we call "the other Deer Hill Road"—just over a ridge opposite our current house. These two roads were once connected and used by old settlers, looping down toward larger longer country roads.

. . . Not sure what I'm retired from. Maybe the day-to-day concern over children or teenagers? But that was drawing to a close even as this book began. Certainly I'm not retiring from the requirements that keep one alive? Keep one writing? There's much to be done in an ongoing way, and to cease would mean a slide into uselessness, chaos or decay.

I'm recalling a snowshoeing episode on this very slope, but two seasons ago, when sliding and floundering into and out of some difficulty or other (with tangles, the ever present fallen trees).—There it might have meant disaster. That time I left no note . . . and the snow was as deep as one might like for a good outing. But I'd made a mistake—or a misadventure. The "mistake" namely of following tracks of deer. You see, I'd found their lying-down places up back of the house. They might have looked down on me from above as they dozed off in late twilight or early starlight. Or, that is, looked down on our tiny log house from their nestling beds in deep deep snow above. Their prints trailed across our neighbor's slope in the opposite direction to that taken by Allen and I yesterday. These neighbors are on the *other side*, more toward the pond at the foot of our narrow road.

Mistake is the wrong word, perhaps. It feels like a mistake during the struggle. The up-and-down, back-and-forth; the climbing over, bending under; all while wearing webbed giant shoes—full of holes to get hooked and send one down, twisted, maybe not to rise again. Or to go on like nothing happened. A little something happened and you've been retrieved. One wallows, limbs *cattawumpus*: too deep to push up, out, without some aid. Once a friend of Allen's dropped unexpectedly into a deep crevice or maybe a old settler's cistern. Down in over his head. He had to dig himself out, *upward*, using one of his snowshoes. With my hips and knees in their current state of slow and painful decay, it's no easy thing to get the shoes off and on. Position is everything and conditions don't always allow for positioning. So *mistake* might be the right word for the adventure . . . but on the other hand . . .

Who knows what a trek will bring? The struggle is a given on these slopes, finding no trail. But the rewards? Best summed up in Edward Abbey's words after one of his desert treks. Lost, maybe injured, maybe struck by the sun, without water or direction; saying over and over: "I'll never do *this* again." But when he is out of it, seeing some recognizable form, some rock ridge, the familiar broken saguaro: a sight of the car by the road. Sitting down next to the car, leaning into it.

Oh.

Oh, can't wait to do that again.

So we set out together, just for a bit of exercise, elevated heart rate, a glimpse of changing sky through the branches of our woodland neighborhood. We choose to get off the snowy tractor trail into thickets because I asked for it, thinking it best to struggle on the way out and come back with more ease on said tractor-broken trail. The rewards will be those we hoped for, mentioned at the start of this paragraph. And later would come the welcome sight of home through trees, the warmth of its woodstove, salad-making, first swallows of ale. The friendliness of Allen grilling some salmon at the gas stove. All this, a pattern of what life sometimes can be. Of what *life is*.

The accretion of snow in a cloud takes place at temperatures of between -40 degrees and 10 degrees. Water vapor collects on dust particles in the air, freezes, and then collects more vapor. This geometric crystallizing, these whirling and drifting heavenly forms . . . this white visitor is the maker of Maine's silent white nights. It muffles winter days and slows or stops our movements for hours, and, on occasion, days.

To add to the mystery, when Maine's mean yearly snowfalls are plotted station by station on a map, some interesting features appear in snow belts. There are six distinct belts, ranging from plus 60 inches on the coast to plus 120 inches in the north. The dam, near the 46th parallel, had the highest yearly mean 123" while Belfast on the coast had the lowest with 61".

Belfast is in the smallest belt lying along our coasts, arcing to include bay coasts of Penobscot, Blue Hill and Frenchman's. The primary coastal snow belt, however, is in the 70's range, extending from Kittery to Eastport, including those bay coasts. Maine's southern interior belt includes snowfalls in the 80's and 90's.

Maine's mountains stretch from her western border to the Katahdin Knot. In this Appalachian tail-end region we find her at her snowiest: snowfalls between 100 and 120 inches. On the map, Ripogenus Dam marks the beginning (in the south), of the snowiest belt, arcing northeastward to Caribou. West of this arc is a blank owing to insufficient data.

Over the entire state, NOAA reports that the greatest snowstorm of the 1951–80 period was 46 inches, at Ripogenus Dam in December of 1962. Even so, Maine averages the most snow in January and snow reaches its maximum depth in February. Maine, is snow king. Of the northeast. (This report of mine was published in Maine Monthly Digest, 1990.)

My previous shoeing (straight up the incline behind our house) put me in mind, again, of my virtual helplessness in the face of such hazards. Yes, when Allen was gone for the day to the coast. I worked around desk and house and then decided to tackle that steep slope. But who was doing the tackling?—me or the mountain?

Ravens called to one another alerting of my presence in woods below. Were they taking verbal notes about my great webbed feet, the poles in my grips as I hauled ass upward towards them? Angling the slight downward-and-across—escaping some fallen tangles—those lengthy limbs and dead trunks—I felt like Olive Oil with her big *big* feet flapping, her long awkward stride—*Oh Popeye!* But mostly I aimed for the uphill, the handhold, the great tree-rest, the miracle of just going *up* instead of sliding, tumbling backwards, possibly becoming one of those frightful tangles myself. It was a miracle, each body length upward the victory, a prayer of thanksgiving . . . with the next reach transmuting the prayer to one of help. *Help me get up this slide here, this extra-steep, this possible knee buster, hip shambler, shoulder dislocator.*

Up up up. Up past the old bear den, and the ever unexpected ledge behind our neighbors'. Every time I see that ledge my thoughts recede in disappointment. Always seems it should be located either higher or lower. Not, as now, right exactly where somehow I *have* to get around through some form of greater exertion. Ice-ridden, snow encrusted implacable rockface.

Brr.

Got to get past that. Please. *Past.*

That means going higher again . . . and behind—over. And through all the tangle, that jutting deadfall. I know there was an old settlers' track up there. Always. If I could find that now!

Is a snowflake a poem in another form? Would it be better to ask . . . is poetry snow falling in another form? True poetry is, of course, form accreted of words, carefully worked. Wendell Berry even makes a good case for "free" poetic *forms* being . . . well, forms. He does this by using likeness to the organic.

Even dust is filled with pattern, especially when the aided eye sees down into its structure—and how much more so on the atomic level? To "atomize" something is to destroy its structure; but, think, electron microscopic structuring itself is not destroyed in so doing. How much more the melting of a snowflake? All its carefully accreted beauty will have disappeared into some other form.

At the turn of the 20th-century, a Vermont farmer—whose careful craftsmanship may not have been appreciated in his little community—revealed the delicacy and intricacy of snowflake formations. As a boy working with microscope, and recording with paper and pencil, Wilson A. Bentley discovered the distinct structural accretion resulting of atmospheric forces around a particle of dust. One hundred years later an electron microscope was sharing with us the fantastic makeup of all the "dust flakes" of our own bodies. If God so dress one of these minute majestic snowflakes . . . which melts away again to constituents—How much more *ye snowshoers,* so carefully and lovingly cast in God's likeness? Oh ye of little faith?

There is some mighty working going on here. We won't let the cynic, a mindset as false as sentimentalism, distract us from our true work: our thinking about this might—mighty workmanship—of God. As I understand, from reading Anne Morrow Lindbergh, cynicism and sentimentalism are tones used in writing and speaking—perhaps presenting a false expression of what is true. These tonal qualities often warn off readers.

But I have loved the romance of snow. The gentle down-pouring, sifting of cold flakes formed with care in the particular atmosphere. These things can be studied and much meditated upon, with loving abstraction, the gaze going outward as all things visible disappear into snowy twilight.

I must locate that old settlers' trail before the twilight comes down on *me.* Maybe sundering me from Allen through mishap in these tangles and snags—but here it is! And now here is the view! Up, above the neighborhood! Up, above the troublesome ledge.

I'm not seeing the neighbors, but barely one or two very small rooftops among bristling trees; more, I'm seeing vapor sifting and shifting, barely perceiving (if at all) its movement between two low mountains, dark with winter's half-light. And yet, in its austerity, as I move on the old track now strewn every-which-way with great deadfall—. This deadfall is great—yet it was not but the gleam in some old oaken or beechen or ashen eye/seed when mountain settlers harked this way to the homestead.

Trudge around the split and pitiful trunks and limbs, descrying again the outline of the track—oh there it is—the clear descent. So dear and crisp and certain . . . but still, I see, a *descent.* Always trouble on the snowy steep. At least the shoes have claws. I have heels, to set back upon—and I still have muscles, tendons, knees—if now less able.

Contrast that encounter with my first recollected encounter with snow . . . So momentous was it to be. Evidently I'd not had the extreme good fortune to see snow before this. My brother was carefully, enthusiastically informing me. Other, loving, hands above me—hands of a giant—clothed me in special garments one needed to meet the snow. My brother, his skin fair, firm and crisp, talked on, my mentor and guide. I was going to meet the snow. Amazing stuffs God himself had made. From heaven where it was specially prepared. (He may have used the word *sky,* but his complete enthusiasm, and promise of what God had made, so transported me that the word *heaven* propelled the rapture of such expectation.) I was going to see *snow*. I would be outside *in snow*!

My next childhood memory is of the actual encounter. Having rightly been prepared for the great moment (—or, was it to be a grave moment?—) I was now clothed and bundled in dim light, outside the house, trying with all my might to see *the snow*.

. . . But the harder I tried . . . the less I saw.

What?!

The snow would not let me see it! Oh the dreadful snow! How am I to see the snow when it keeps getting in my eyes?! Is this the grave and blissful stuff told me? This stuff that won't let you even *see*?! God has tricked me!

Next memory with regard to snow: wallowing under my baby sister's crib rolling, whining. Thundering mad *at the personal Snow Maker*.

Yes, I believed then in God. In fact I believed far more, I think, than now. And God knew my thoughts and that I knew he'd tricked me! With the snow! How *could* You?

But, I'm over it now.

But here's Allen, now passing; now up ahead, his shoulders dark against a darker dimming of snowy woodland at day's end. He's smaller now in my gaze; the woodland larger . . . as he has gone on . . . breaking trail. The track isn't so hard against my painful foot, pain sustained after the ancient ice storm, plantar fascia never healing.

We are companions, helping one another.

One another, loving. Still and wholly learning what it is to love. The breaking, mending, breaking. Often learning feels like fragmentation, like fragments coming in fragments, bits and pieces, bytes and particles, the shivering fall in love.

It's a bit like watching, (imaginatively) experiencing God's painful un-making of the world, slowly, almost softly, sometimes shimmery, shivering to tatters, fragments. Where once upon a time God had been building it up. Just so. And with colossal painstaking effort. Such effort that we cannot imagine.

But God sees to that imaginative dearth as well. Thus, God gives me my own little piece in creation's production and dismantling. In its tender incremental making, unmaking, remaking. In its life, in its death, in its resurrection.

Courage. Take. Eat. This is my Body. Open your mouth. Hold out your tongue. Cold and fresh. Now melting.—It's a delicately intricately individually made snowflake.

. . . You know, snow . . .

February 28, 2013

The days are longer; still, cabin fever persists. We live in the mountains of Western Maine where snowfall is plentiful and deep, occasionally yet falling.

Snowshoeing this a.m. passed neighbors,' up and beyond. We have followed deer tracks in deep snow, and they have followed our snowshoe trails. They move in twilight hours. We are invisible, so are they. Theirs is a stronger scent than ours yet they smell us better than we do them. I find out their lie-down places sometimes, individual oval hollows in the snow. We never meet, though I've spied some moving among trees, slow and stopping—up above the house, from my study window. They are camo-dark shapes.

We test a snow-covered stream before crossing. They have no need to test. Especially when snow is crusty, icy, snow-walking is hard on their tender feet and what we'd call their ankles. These are not real ankles but part of the foot above "toes," actual split hooves. They walk on their toes, two toes—a cloven hoof. We see trails behind these deep twin holes, where dew claws of bucks drag, delicately. Distinctly. Their hooves are more splayed; does' are more pointed heart-shaped, together.

The snow this a.m. is heavy, wet and deep. It sticks to our pole-tips and steel bear claws underneath the rawhide webbing of wide shoes. In winter you are free of defined woodland trails and most bugs, and you don't get lost (or "turned around," as they say), in the woods—because when you are tired you can go back on your track, following it home. So you don't need paths in winter. And it's exhilarating to move through softly snowed small beeches. You need only keep twigs out of your eyes. Some of these tips are reddening, and, today, coated delicately in snow. The trail is pure and white, patterning, a thread weaving through trees ancient and girthy, mighty and tall. Weaving up-and-down slope where small snowy streams have cut ravines. Or spindly, delicately patterning these white woods where your breath comes visible, puffy and misty as snow—mists . . . but your own.

About The Old Settlers' Well (February 6, 2014)

You know we live under a ridge in a narrow vale along which we snow-shoe. This is a mountainous u-shaped valley with dead-end road but once extending up the low mountainside to meet another road in these hills. Set-tlers actually drove wagons between rugged slopes. Don't know how they did it. Anyway, it's all wooded now and you can see the old ruts they made. Saplings grow in them. Sometimes, in three seasons, if I've "got turned around in woods" (as they say) and I come on one of these mostly hidden tracks, I have a feeling of gratitude, and can follow along until I come to an ATV trail, stream, or road.

In woods are old cellar holes, some with pretty girthy trees growing in them. And tons of old stone walls crisscrossing on abandoned slopes. Of course logging's ongoing so trees are of various size in sections of the slopes. And sometimes you see open sky over nothing but downed limbs, abandoned, trunks, etc . . . With new growth coming up between. Walking can be difficult when once-recognized trails are obliterated.

But the neat thing about snowshoeing, as mentioned before—you don't need a trail. Especially when the snow is deep—as it falls in these mountains sometimes. And shoeing off-track will not get you lost because, if you traipse into unfamiliar territory, you can always follow back on your webbed trail—if it's not covered deep in new snowfall. I'm seldom out long enough for that.

Deer tracks crisscross over snow. So many tracks on open areas (limited in this narrow valley), and all through these woods. Tracks are cloven in snow. Bucks have longer hairs behind, just above their hooves, marking fresh deep snow. In places where they've lain snow melts from the warmth of their bodies. Sometimes you see leaves under a skim of ice where they've slept. I was hoping for more snow so we can get out more and yesterday—snowing!

But about the old settlers' well . . .

We've discovered an old settlers spring fed well not far from our house. Surprisingly we've never noticed it before. It's above a stream running un-der ice and snow, dug out long ago and lined with stones; and the stones are green and mossy, but the spring is still gurgling in . . . then trickling, filtering down to a stream at the foot of these wooded properties.

We have another survivalist friend with many skills who tells us such a find can be made to supply clean fresh water, adding that it's most neces-sary to survival in any situation. He says that the contamination of water could conceivably end life on Earth, then suggests a particular method of rehabilitating this old dug well that will secure its use for irrigation, prevent animals from befouling it, enable groundwater to refill; to purify. He has done such work himself in the woods, using a plastic culvert to fit tightly inside keeping rocks from tumbling inward. He poured in 50 lbs. of sandbox sand purchased at Home Depot, then used the shocking process with bleach for purification.

Moose Tracks (February 21, 2014)

On snowshoes we followed what I thought were moose tracks in deep snow. We hadn't seen a moose in the valley or neighborhood in several years . . . although we did see one with huge rack, browsing, and cooling himself, in the south pond summer before last. That was the time of year one can also see the flying flag of a white-tail deer as it leaps through woods to escape the interloper. But I've never seen a deer do so against a background of fresh snow.

The snow is deep at last—nearer the end of the season but we have it gladly. Skiers come for it of course, and resort businesses depend on it. But these tracks—the length of the creature's stride! White and deep, the double dip at the front for a cloven hoof. Had no camera with us, but don't think any photo of mine would do these tracks justice.

Deer tracks were trailing along the slope above and behind our house when we started out on a track broken behind a neighboring house. We swap off breaking trail with deer. We break in daylight, and they follow it during the night. Sometimes it's the reverse. They break and so we have it easier. But we don't leave droppings for them to step in. We don't eat the bark off slender moose maples, a.k.a. Norway maples.

When we came down a snowy abandoned drive to the road and crossed over (after a spot of conversation with a stranger in a car about a body buried in concrete and its place in neighborhood lore). We went into woods on the opposite side, much tangled in places, dark stems in white ground, and kept straight following dark red splotches on tree trunks—the property line of ??—don't know. Maybe timber, paper company, or potential developer? Or could it be Mert's marker? Anyway, we followed to the brook. We wanted to meander on home with it, the same brook crossing under the road, then flowing along the front of our property. God's property. Yes, we really believe he's got us using it for now, though there's paper and records saying we "own" it.

So we followed this, its surface frozen in snow cover, with black and open water here and there. Its bank deep and snowy and sometimes cut with deer tracks made since our last thick fall of snow.

Then we saw the moose tracks! *What stride*, I kept saying. That depth and width. And so fresh! Allen wondered over that. And he thought it possible . . .

Maybe it wasn't a moose. Moose are gigantic deer with great snouts, dim eyes and huge palmate antlers (the males). Male and female are peaceable unless hurt, in the rut, or have young with them. Still, you may or may not want to see one of these great beings in the woods. I've written elsewhere of seeing one giant dreaming by the roadside . . . possibly awaiting his autumnal mate. Mighty sight! If not for that numb look in his eye, you would think him a sovereign.

Allen was thinking these tracks very fresh, their edges crisp, not eroded. And . . . might they not be leapings? Deer tracks, not moose . . . and not far in front of us, this creature? And us spooking it along? We are noisy in the woods. The deep snow makes a muffled *whomping* when people-weight collapses its underlying structure. The first time we heard it I mistook it for a tree falling in the distance. Plus, we talk sometimes. "This way." "Watch the eye level twigs." "Too steep here." And the like.

We follow these tracks. What a stride. What—leaping? We watched for the telltale clue. And then we saw it. The normal deer stride connecting these tracks to another apparently longer stride. Meaning, a deer had been spooked by the snow-shoers and then thought it had shaken them, reconsidered with the help of its deer ears, and gone on at a leap.

Leaping.

I wish I might have seen a leaping deer. A white-tale deer, its white tail signaling. Trying hard to escape us through dark trees against a bright background of snow.

Coyote and Deer (a week or so later)

The day before, just as we were coming up the drive after snowshoeing, an eagle flew over our house. Bald eagle. This hasn't happened before—we don't see them much here. It was grand! Head and tail white, wings brown and giant, spread in flight. I had heard ravens calling earlier, on the wooded slope above, to the east.

We went shoeing up there along the same route as in the last entry, but this time—were those droppings?—bright, reddish—berries?! Had a deer been eating berries . . . out of season . . . to make red droppings? Surely the color would have gone.—Vomit, maybe?!

I went closer on snowshoes. Then saw clumps of fur. Dense clumps, reddish, lots of red on the white icy snow, beneath tangles of dark twigs and limbs above. I stared down at the fur—like a heavy fur coat ripped to tufts.

Coyotes! Must have taken a deer. Two?

Coyote pack? I shoe past with care, thinking. Neighborhood domestic dogs on the loose? They might have killed, but not gorged. Further along, I look back. I had already called Allen's attention to those bloodied clumps of fur. So strange. I'd seen hide and bits of bones before but not like this, savaged. Those had been the more orderly leavings of poachers. Human beings behaving unlawfully. These, back of me now as I went toward the neighbors', were leavings of lawful savagery. Nature devouring her own.

Then, looking back, further down-slope from where Allen was passing, I saw more. A wash of red, rich in the white snow-cover. There—most of a deer, feasted on, devoured. I did not go down that way to investigate but Allen was bound to be curious about tracks surrounding it. For one thing, we could see the roof of our house from here. The same roof over which an eagle had flown the day before. The death and feasting with canine tooth-and-claw had occurred between our neighbors' and that roof, in the midst of the lot between.

He'd be sorry to have no camera with him. I'd been about to grab mine before leaving the house but neglected it. Not that I'd been wanting visual evidence of bloody wild gluttony. But to puzzle out the tracks—that would be worthy. I have a track booklet at home. Allen, however, went to eyeball them, then he came on ahead toward me over the shoed trail, still puzzled.

Listening to his description, I thought well-defined claws would justify the canine pair, canine pack. He however could not distinguish *well-defined*. Looking around me as we went on, eyeing tracks over the icy and darkly pocked surface, I noticed deep deer, but also the light cat track, and thought about the bobcat, the lynx, I'd scared up from under the flight of porch stairs the other night returning home in the dark. If the slain was a small deer—not even a yearling? Couldn't the fat cat with fur, thick tufted cheeks, have got herself (himself?) an eight, nine-month-old fawn?

Maybe.

Now Allen was talking of getting a varmint gun. A sheathed bobcat knife for his belt? Me, I so loved going alone in the woods. We've got bow-and-arrows but I can't see myself getting good with bows and arrows. Not like our forebears. And I can't really picture me/varmint gun. Maybe a der-ringer? Bear spray?

I will leave it, after all, to the hunters. They shoot not only deer (in season) but coyotes—anytime. Because, thank God, coyotes are legal in coyote season. And their season is January 1 to December 31.

Coyotes, you see, go after the deer . . . cutting into Maine's seasonal deer supply.

But about those bobcat. Have you ever heard one? When they go off at night in the listening woods (or anywhere, anytime); screaming *bob-bob-bob!!!*, a bit like a possessed human. The other Deer Hill Road neighbor kids ran inside, slammed the door, after hearing that come up through the woods. I'd hate to leave fawns to bobcat—but not so much to the coyote. Nor the poacher.

Because, you know, we could get shot in the woods.

But that would be all right, I guess. I'd forgive a hunter. With the coyote attacking me . . . would there be anything to forgive?

. . . Guessing now that I understand better why that deer was spooked the other day as we went through a wooded section by the stream on our snowshoes. It must have heard us coming, *whumping* over the snow. And took off. Leaping. Leaping.

New Year between Mountains and The Gulf

(We cycle back out of old age to the book's beginning)

"*If I take the wings of the morning, and dwell in the uttermost parts of the sea . . .*"

Words. I summon words as we roar into thin air on our New Year's flight from the Oxford Hills toward Mount Desert Island in the Gulf of Maine. (Or do these words summon me?)

Allen is flying into the north shortly after nine a.m., me noting Streaked (pronounced Streak-ked) and Singepole Mountains, landmarks and guides by which I judge our ascent and descent. They've been my friends and comforters on more local flights that increase Allen's ability, and his credited hours aloft. Now our path curves into the east. We are extending our range—and, looking out again, I see mellow gold light lying upon the distant sea off my right shoulder. The sun itself is unseen, owing to broken cloud layer at higher elevations. That bright patch on distant sea is a great pool of molten light, maybe twenty-five miles in length, maybe fifty; who can say? Not I.

Immediate but vague metaphoric intimations about this pool; yet I suspect it will be but a brief and glorious show. A morning phenomenon, quickly fading.

Unusual conditions today: a surface wind of zero knots, while winds aloft at 3000' will be 19 knots from the northwest. Scattered clouds at 10,000'. The outside thermometer above our instrument panel reads 5 degrees. We're on a magnetic compass heading of due east to the Augusta VOR, where we'll change course to 95 degrees for the Bar Harbor area. Destination: Hancock County Airport, on New Years Day.

The Oxford Hills, my comforting landmarks, have sunk back, along with Little Singepole and Streaked Mountains. Vague blueness northward holds the constant fixed column of International Paper smoke. A fixture among hills night and day, as though standing forever unmoving. Toward the east a crenellated wall of terrain—blue, in appearance barring our flight path—the Camden Hills, hedging our horizon.

Three groups of trees seen from heaven. One group passing directly below, the neatness and precision of a miniscule apple orchard: centrality of form in its youngest trees make a complete pattern reminiscent of meristem tissue (from the Greek for a portion of warp on a loom). An undifferentiated cell structure forming into what it shall be as new tissue arises. Seen from above the pattern's a microcosm of making. Another group is passing below on the bristling snowy floor of deciduous forest. I would see any largish creature (say a deer) chancing among those twigs. Twigs they appear from this heavenly height. Not so with the next group . . . now passing below—conifers. From the ground, conifers appear mysterious; yet, when seen from this perspective, they produce no inscrutable yearning in me. But, when earth-bound, on seeing such firs—dark, lined above me upon a desolate ridge somewhere—I can be greatly moved. Whence comes the power trees hold upon a kindled imagination?

Allen, monitoring Augusta traffic, breaks my reverie. Deafening engine noise and malfunctioning earphones. I holler my query and he points out a distant cone—the VOR or omni, source of navigational signals—on the white field of the airport. The end of this airfield is artificially elevated above surrounding terrain. Because of its size and construction, it has the peculiar distinction of looking it once geological and man-made. We roar over the VOR . . . the indicator flips . . . our heading is now 95 degrees.

Passing over the state capital, I find Kennebec River siphoning off my attention; distracting from sights of the Capitol dome and blocky buildings, so many toy blocks where legislation and policy are puzzled through. Something is pulling on me. I search a geographical puzzle where Kennebec River snakes southwestward toward The Gulf in flat curves of frozen sheen. There below, in spots where Kennebec flows wet, I see clouds quickly passing in its unfrozen depths. But my gaze is drawn far out—to the sea. To a vast golden spot, still there!—Fixed!

But no . . . not fixed . . . As I watch with attention, the spot holds an island, now two. The great glorious spot is moving across stationary islands, transforming them momently with light and then passing on. This grant of the sun has finally penetrated my watchful attentiveness: We are moving together in parallel. Muscongus Bay—gifted with sun's presence, the sun, which I cannot directly see for the cloud. I look. Then look away in distracted joy. . . . The light moves on!

Camden Hills, fast approaching, taking on the appearance of waves. Waves of solid land. Have seen this before, in other glaciated hills. Ancient snow giants sheared southeastern faces, leaving rock crests. Land, green-brown, like mighty frozen waves forever poised, threatening to crash. I saw them like this from summer's perch on Milan Hill's fire tower in New Hampshire—in that line of hills approaching the Berlin pluton from behind. But first, we saw them so on the neighboring east road, near the landlord's house where we dwell. These Camden Hills passing appear mightier than the sea. Towering above Penobscot Bay, they are a leading edge of the ponderous ocean of earth. A massive dual wave of earth-rock, cresting. But a moment—they will crash! Crash into the thin paltry light-soaked sea.

Cold legs and numb feet. Light glinting off Allen's glasses. He smiles, pulls the knob designated *cabin heat*. But it makes no difference. Vented off the manifold, this is no true heat. Sit long in one stiff position, with legs drawn up to keep feet off co-pilot rudder pedals. If Allen had a heart attack we'd fall into the bay.

Now! An arrow, a bar of gold, moving on sea. We cross the border of land and bay. Gold shoots toward us on water. The arrow of light, pushing, nudging beneath our craft.

Look directly but briefly at this light. Distant on our trip, it's now up under our wing, blinding. Cannot see for this mass of light! Ah, here peripheral vision is the thing. A hasty glance back. The mass of *bright* (lingering yet on the Gulf of Maine) has thrown out its strong shaft of blinding silver-white. One quick unresisting direct look: now I see a fainter rippling along the shaft's edge. And look away.

Oh that radiant companion from the sea, from the sun. Like so much in nature, it leads me to think of *greater*. Nature coupled with creative thinking leading to mystical realms. These quietly insistent natural wonders are harbingers of another world. In this case, surely a lighter world. So light I cannot now look at it.

We cross Blue Bay. The snow is gone. Earth, beneath our wings, is light brown. Fields are wide, open. Blue Hill, to the right of craft's nose, is a dark blue bump, passing. My attention is now riveted on dim mountains beyond. The hazy great mountains of Mount Desert; massive, profound above seas.

The Hobbs meter indicates we've been a good hour in air. Hancock County radio indicates an active runway, 4. We locate the tiny strip and Allen begins banking for approach. *Even there shalt thy hand lead me.*

Turning, we face into hazy gold. At sea, between clefts of Mount Desert mountains, is the distant bowl of molten gold. In every swatch of water shines its outpour, spilling inland. Blinding brightness follows in all streams, ponds, inlets. Gold and silver so bright in my eyes it leaves negative squiggles on the page where feverishly I set these notes. The shape of these images is that of whatever body of water I saw last. Ah, there is the deep distant bowl of gold. In our flight straight toward it, it appears motionless, full. *Generous.*

Some eighty years before our late 1980's—from this dramatic setting—a sloop, supplemented with two gasoline engines, began sailing Gulf of Maine coasts. According to Dorothy Simpson's *The Maine Islands in Story and Legend,* the *Sunbeam* sailed all weather into isolated coves, to islands and islets, holding clinics, carrying education, entertainment and morale to lonely coastal inhabitants. From Kittery to Quoddy Head came the *Sunbeam* with interest and encouragement. An intrepid crew; with them in the islanders' sickness and health, at the moment of birth, the moment of death: For every state of human condition, the *Sunbeam,* and successively, *Sunbeams II* and *III* were there into the 1940's. Shore communities are now connected by roads; some islands are linked by ferry or bridge. The services and friendship, as of a spirit of the sloop, is still spilling its gold around.

Our craft's flaps are down, the runway increasing in size, perspective expanding it as we descend. A smooth, rolling touchdown on tarmac. Bleared, am looking around for a ramp leading to a terminal. Itching ears; removing my headphones, rub my ears to relax them. The sea wind blows as I struggle from our craft. Coffee, please. Hot coffee. But it's New Year's Day. The coffee bar in this terminal is gated and dark. . . .

We sit in the mostly deserted terminal, still wrapped in our coats, verbally exploring the possibilities, but without a vehicle nothing avails. We must be content with hours logged, the true purpose of the flight. So it's back to the plane.

Our new heading is 275 degrees west, back to Augusta, 270 back to Oxford. Allen tunes the Bangor ATIS solely for something to listen to. He primes the engine, turns the key. The craft explodes to life, its blue artificial horizon and compass bobbing. "Cessna 23 Juliet, back taxiing on runway 4 . . . Departing runway 4." A rush down the tarmac. The runway dwindles beneath our polished wings, is gone.

Below: delicate white-limned shoreline of Western Bay. All things look delicate, fragile with increased altitude. The earth is a Christmas ornament (filigreed and fragile), as in the words from outer space of one astronaut. Waters away from us are blue; yet those, directly below, green. Cross the big bay. Then, a large circular patch of reddish peat—2,300 feet. Approach Blue Hill, southern slope on my right, sides sloping, reddish, a blue crown of tiny conifers upon its head of rock. Small, isolated, perfect round head.

Thermometer, 5 degrees. Air leaks in; am very cold, stiff. We fly without words, muffled in the noise of our craft, each in a fragile world of varying but intense observation: Allen for his instruments and other, occasional, craft; I for sights, and insights.

Long I watch the northward view . . . Slowly . . . becoming aware of something following alongside upon the distant ground. Barely perceptible. So slight that I wonder if something is truly there . . . I *do* see it! Zipping along in silence, as though our accompanying shadow. Yet it is no shadow, but a strange amorphous light.

Is that us? I mouth the words to Allen, pointing.

He, joking: *It's our anti shadow.*

Later, in reading, I will discover that the bright traveling spot is indeed solar- related to the craft's shadow. I noted the shape and size of our shadow, on an earlier flight, changing according to the plane's distance from the earth on which it is cast. The higher we go, the smaller and less plane-shaped it becomes, losing its terrestrial and man-made shape. The shadow becomes diamond-shaped then circular, like the shape of our light-source itself. The higher we fly, the more sun-shaped we become. According to Dr. Elizabeth Wood in her book, *Science for the Airplane Passenger*, the bright spot actually surrounds our slowly diminishing shadow. Thus, as we draw ever nearer the sun, increasing brightness overtakes it completely.

We share the skies between Penobscot Bay and the Kennebec Valley with other pilots. I watch two white planes, one behind the other, take off from Belfast. Airplanes below are always crisply white, clean-looking, against the ground—according to Dr. Wood, an effect of lower atmosphere, cluttered with light-scattered particles. On this flight we see white planes moving against dark trees at lower altitudes; above we see dark flying cross-shapes. Below, above: our position determines which we see. Another we see way out towards The Gulf, like a big black gnat moving silently across beclouded sky. Here's one! not dark, with sun glinting off, a scant 500 ft. above our heads! Cutting across our heading, the pilot's sunglasses clearly visible. I gape at his nearness, audacity . . . *And thy right hand shall hold me.*

Am growing stiff, hungry, trance-like. Hunker down over my state of observation, entrenched. Owl-like, turning my head, see in the north that unmistakable telltale column of paper mill smoke, piled, stationary, into sky. Maybe Scott Paper on the Kennebec? Turn my head back again. Off in the furthest distance, hills—Oxford Hills?—against the backdrop of New Hampshire whites. Sky there is darkening, full of cloud down to the horizon.

But what of the traveling gold upon the sea, our companion?

It has closed up, become but a thin distant line, a creepy crepuscular light in the sky to our left; and dim lines of light in cloud overlaying yet one thin thread of gold. Land around this light lies in colorless bunches.

Here and there ice upon a pond; directly below is gray and lacy white, a snowy pattern. Kennebec passes, frozen, silent; and that stationary column on my right. Augusta is gone, with its airport chatter. The West, where we are headed, is darkening, drearily hazy, and dim. I am numb with cold and hunger, my mind a somnambulant glaze of thoughtlessness. My pencil sleep-walks on the cards. Now the line of gold is almost gone. The somber landscape dulls me. Dimness lies over all land, and upon my thought.

There is some question . . . in the droning, vibrating sleepiness . . . about . . . Some question of where is the Oxford airport . . . But I, the visual navigator, do not know. What land mark? What hills are these we fly toward? Allen says something about landing on Thompson Lake. Should I be caring? . . .

But suddenly I see *the gold* once more—lively, bright—moving across an inland lake. I wake, seeing this golden sign below, deep, recognizing its significance. This apparent shining-deep-beneath-lakes will travel on forever. Gliding from lake to stream to sea and back. As though a great globe of light stationary beneath Maine's gleaming rotating surface. It shines up from below; as though moving under *glass.* Glass: Our fragile earth.

Now I'm awake. Those hills to our right must be Oxford's, foothills of the Whites! One of those four—distinct, rounded—will be Streaked Mountain.

Yes, I know this place, these uncanny eastern sides of hills now so *unfamiliar*. The backsides of our own home hills.

I had not seen them from this direction, this outer space, before.

www.ingramcontent.com/pod-product-compliance
Lightning Source LLC
Chambersburg PA
CBHW061733050726
47598CB00002B/470